The Open University

Mathematics Foundation Course Unit 7

SEQUENCES AND LIMITS I

Prepared by the Mathematics Foundation Course Team

Correspondence Text 7

The Open University Press

Open University courses provide a method of study for independent learners through an integrated teaching system including textual material, radio and television programmes and short residential courses. This text is one of a series that make up the correspondence element of the Mathematics Foundation Course.

The Open University's courses represent a new system of university level education. Much of the teaching material is still in a developmental stage. Courses and course materials are, therefore, kept continually under revision. It is intended to issue regular up-dating notes as and when the need arises, and new editions will be brought out when necessary.

Further information on Open University courses may be obtained from The Admissions Office, The Open University, P.O. Box 48, Bletchley, Buckinghamshire.

The Open University Press
Walton Hall. Bletchley, Bucks

First Published 1970
Copyright © 1970 The Open University

Printed in Great Britain by
J W Arrowsmith Ltd, Bristol 3

SBN 335 01006 7

Contents

Objectives

The general aim of this text is to introduce the idea of a limit as applied to sequences and to functions. After working through this unit, you should be able to:

(i) write down the definition of the limit of
    (a) an infinite sequence,
    (b) a real function for large numbers in its domain,
    (c) a real function near a number a;

(ii) explain what is meant by a function being continuous at a number a in its domain;

(iii) determine whether simple sequences and functions have limits and evaluate these limits, when they exist;

(iv) reproduce and use the results on the sum, product and functions of convergent sequences;

(v) evaluate the limits of sequences defined by recurrence formulas of the type $u_k = F(u_{k-1})$, when these limits exist;

(vi) understand the connection between the exponential function and growth and decay processes;

(vii) write down the definitions of the exponential and natural logarithm functions;

(viii) write down the exponential theorem.

N.B.
Before working through this correspondence text, make sure you have read the general introduction to the mathematics course in the Study Guide, as this explains the philosophy underlying the whole course. You should also be familiar with the section which explains how a text is constructed and the meanings attached to the stars and other symbols in the margin, as this will help you to find your way through the text.

Structural Diagram

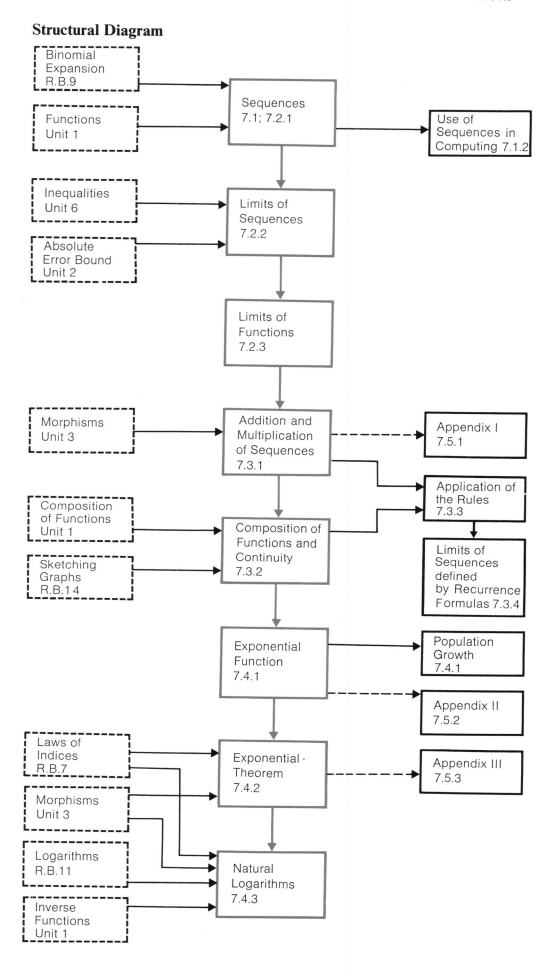

Glossary

Terms which are defined in this glossary are printed in CAPITALS.

LIMIT OF A FUNCTION f NEAR A POINT a	A LIMIT OF A FUNCTION f NEAR A POINT a is a number L such that, for any positive number ε, however small, there is a positive number δ such that the set $\{x : 0 < |x - a| \leqslant \delta$ and $x \in$ the domain of $f\}$ is non-empty, and its image under f is a subset of $[L - \varepsilon, L + \varepsilon]$.	25, 30
LIMIT OF AN INFINITE SEQUENCE	A LIMIT OF AN INFINITE SEQUENCE is a number L such that, for every interval centred on L, there is an ELEMENT of the sequence after which every element belongs to the interval.	12, 19
NATURAL LOGARITHM FUNCTION	The NATURAL LOGARITHM FUNCTION is the inverse of the EXPONENTIAL FUNCTION.	53
NATURAL NUMBERS, THE SEQUENCE OF	The SEQUENCE OF NATURAL NUMBERS is the SEQUENCE of the positive integers, arranged in their natural order.	4
NEWTON'S METHOD FOR SQUARE ROOTS	NEWTON'S METHOD FOR SQUARE ROOTS is a method for calculating $\sqrt{a}$ $(a \in R^+)$, by SUCCESSIVE APPROXIMATIONS based on the RECURRENCE FORMULA $$u_k = \frac{1}{2}\left(u_{k-1} + \frac{a}{u_{k-1}}\right).$$	5
REAL FUNCTION	A REAL FUNCTION is a function whose domain and codomain are both R or subsets of R.	23
RECURRENCE FORMULA	A RECURRENCE FORMULA is a formula expressing each ELEMENT in a SEQUENCE in terms of its predecessor (or predecessors).	7
SEQUENCE	A SEQUENCE is a set of objects arranged in a definite order. See also FINITE SEQUENCE and INFINITE SEQUENCE.	3, 10
SUCCESSIVE APPROXIMATIONS, SEQUENCE OF	A SEQUENCE OF SUCCESSIVE APPROXIMATIONS is a sequence whose elements are successively better approximations to some number, and such that *any* desired accuracy is achieved by taking a large enough number of elements of the sequence.	5

Notation

The symbols are presented in the order in which they appear in the text.

Z^+	The set of all positive integers.	10
$\underline{u}$	The sequence $u_1, u_2, u_3, \ldots$.	12
$\lim \underline{u}$	The limit of the sequence $\underline{u}$.	12
ε	The absolute error bound for an approximation.	17
$[a, b]$	The interval $\{x : x \in R, a \leqslant x \leqslant b\}$.	17
R^+	The set of all positive real numbers.	23
$\lim\limits_{x \text{ large}} f(x)$	The limit of f for large numbers in its domain.	24
$\lim\limits_{x \to a} f(x)$	The limit of f near the point a.	25
$\underline{u} + \underline{v}$	The sequence $u_1 + v_1, u_2 + v_2, u_2 + v_3, \ldots$ where $\underline{u}$ is the sequence $u_1, u_2, u_3, \ldots$ and $\underline{v}$ is the sequence $v_1, v_2, v_3, \ldots$.	31
$\underline{u} \times \underline{v}$	The sequence $u_1 \times v_1, u_2 \times v_2, u_3 \times v_3, \ldots$ where $\underline{u}$ and $\underline{v}$ are as above.	33
$g(\underline{u})$	The sequence $g(u_1), g(u_2), g(u_3), \ldots$ where $\underline{u}$ is given above and g is a real function.	35
$\simeq$	"is approximately equal to"	48
e	$e = \exp(1) = 2.71828 \ldots$.	50
$\exp$	The exponential function defined by $\exp : x \longmapsto \lim\limits_{k \text{ large}} \left(1 + \dfrac{x}{k}\right)^k$ ($x \in R$ and $k \in Z^+$).	50
$\ln$	The natural logarithm function, which is the inverse of the exponential function.	53

Bibliography

R. Courant and H. Robbins, *What is Mathematics?* (Oxford University Press 1941).

Pages 289–312 give a first-class discussion of the definitions of a limit and of continuity. If you have doubts about these definitions after working through this correspondence text, you are strongly recommended to consult Courant and Robbins.

S. K. Stein, *Calculus for the Natural and Social Sciences*, (McGraw-Hill 1968).

This is a good choice if you feel you need a textbook for the calculus parts of this course (i.e. sequences and limits, differentiation and integration), and do not intend to take any more mathematics after the foundation course. The book has plenty of diagrams, exercises and applications, and is intended to appeal to natural and social scientists particularly. The material of this unit is treated in Chapter 3.

A. H. Lightstone, *Concepts of Calculus I*, (Harper and Row 1965).

This book is somewhat more advanced in its level of treatment than the one by Stein and it is a good choice if you intend to take more mathematics after the foundation course. Its philosophy and notation are similar to those of this course: the aim is to base calculus on the concept of a set and the concept of a limit. Limits of sequences are treated in Chapter 4 and the limit of a function near a point is treated in the first three sections of Chapter 7.

7.0 INTRODUCTION

This unit is the first in a group of six related units (*Sequences and Limits I and II, Integration I and II, Differentiation I and II*), which will introduce you to the branch of mathematics known as *calculus*. This branch of mathematics provides a method of dealing with situations in which we have two related functions such that the images under one of them correspond to rates of change of the images under the other. For example, the velocity of a moving body (regarded as the image of the time under a suitable function) is the same thing as the rate at which its position (also regarded as the image of the time under a suitable function) is changing; so whenever we wish to relate the velocity of a body to its position we may use calculus. The method will be explained in *Unit 12, Differentiation I*.

Calculus is valuable in many applications of mathematics; in particular, it is extremely useful in providing convenient formulations of laws of physical science. Perhaps the best known of these is Newton's second law of motion, which he used to show that the orbits of the planets are ellipses; this law states that the acceleration of a body (the *rate of change* of its velocity), multiplied by its mass, is equal to the total force acting on the body. Calculus is also used in a wide range of non-physical applications; for example, it can be used in economics to formulate the rate at which the profit from a business enterprise varies as its level of activity varies, or in psychology to formulate the rate at which a person forgets things he has recently learned.

Calculus is also concerned with a group of problems of which the simplest (discussed in *Unit 9, Integration I*) is the calculation of the area of the part of a plane bounded by a curve whose equation is known. Some methods for finding these areas were known to the Greeks, but it was not until about 300 years ago that Newton and Leibniz founded the subject of calculus by (independently) discovering the intimate relationship between this problem of calculating areas and the problem of evaluating the rate of change of images under a function. We shall look at this relationship in *Unit 13, Integration II*.

To get some idea of the type of mathematics that we shall need as a basis for calculus, let us consider just what we mean by the "rate of change" of the images under a function. For example, the position of a car moving north on a straight road out of London may be specified fairly closely by giving its distance from its initial position (Westminster say). This distance depends on time: let us denote it by $f(t)$, where t is the time that has elapsed since the car left London at (say) noon. If we know the function f, how do we calculate the velocity*, that is, the rate of change of $f(t)$?

It is easy enough to calculate the *average* velocity of the car over some specified time interval; it is the distance travelled in that time interval divided by the duration of the interval. For example, if the car travels 11 miles in 10 minutes, then its average velocity over this time interval is $\frac{11}{\frac{1}{6}} = 66$ mile/h (since 10 minutes $= \frac{1}{6}$ hour). This rule for calculating average velocities can be written as a formula:

$$\text{average velocity} = \frac{x_2 - x_1}{t_2 - t_1} = \frac{f(t_2) - f(t_1)}{t_2 - t_1}$$

Equation (1)
* * *

where t_1 and t_2 are the times since noon at the beginning and end of the time interval respectively, and $x_1 = f(t_1)$, $x_2 = f(t_2)$ are the distances from London at the beginning and end of the time interval respectively.

---

* "Velocity" means speed in a known direction. Here only two directions are possible: away from London and towards it. We distinguish them by giving the velocity a positive sign for motion away from London, and a negative sign for motion towards it.

In many cases, however, the really important velocity is not the average velocity but the *instantaneous* velocity.

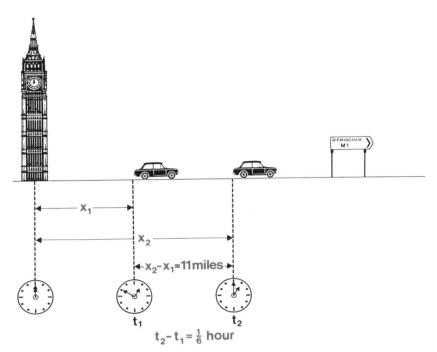

Suppose for example that the car had a collision; then the velocity of vital importance to the occupants of the car is its velocity at the instant of impact, not its average over the previous ten minutes, or even the previous ten seconds, during which the driver may have been braking violently. The obvious way to try to get instantaneous velocities from Equation (1) is to consider a time interval of vanishing duration, that is, to set $t_2 = t_1$. Since the distance travelled by the car in this zero time interval is zero, the fraction in Equation (1) now takes the form $\frac{0}{0}$; this expression, however, is nonsense because there is no mathematically consistent way of defining division by zero. By making $(t_2 - t_1)$ small we can calculate the average velocity over as short a time interval as we please, but as soon as we try to catch the instantaneous velocity by making this time interval exactly zero, the quantity we are looking for slips from our grasp.

In order to catch this elusive fish (assuming, of course, that it really exists), a more sophisticated technique is necessary, in which we deduce the instantaneous velocity from the average velocities over very short time intervals. The technique involves finding the *limit* for very small values of $(t_2 - t_1)$. Before we can understand how to find instantaneous velocities, therefore, we must first understand the concept of a limit, and it is the purpose of the present unit to explain this concept.

Another place where the concept of a limit is useful is in the theory of successive approximation procedures. For example, in the television component of this unit we consider a procedure giving successively better approximations to one of the solutions of the cubic equation $x = \frac{1}{5}(x^3 + 3)$. The first three successive approximations obtained in a particular application of this procedure are 0.5, 0.625, 0.648828; further approximations can be calculated using the formula $u_k = \frac{1}{5}(u_{k-1}^3 + 3)$, ($k = 1, 2, \ldots$) where u_k denotes the kth approximation. None of the members of this sequence is the exact solution of the cubic, yet the sequence does stand in a very special relationship to the solution: the numbers in it are approximations to the solution in the same sense that average velocities over short time intervals are approximations to an instantaneous velocity. To define this relationship precisely, we again need the concept of a limit.

The purpose of this unit is to explain just what we mean by "limit" in mathematics, both in the context of sequences and in the context of functions. Since the concept is somewhat simpler when applied to sequences, we consider sequences first.

7.1   SEQUENCES

7.1.1   What a Sequence is

You have already met sequences informally several times, particularly in *Unit 4, Finite Differences*. At that stage we could treat the properties of sequences as intuitively obvious and so we did not need any strict mathematical definition of the term "sequence"; it was enough to use the word in its everyday sense. Now, however, we shall be using sequences as the foundation for the structure necessary for a definition of limits, and so it is important to be absolutely clear what we mean by the word.

By a sequence we mean a set of objects (not necessarily all different) arranged in a definite order. As examples of sequences we may take:

(i) A line of four cars waiting at a red traffic light:

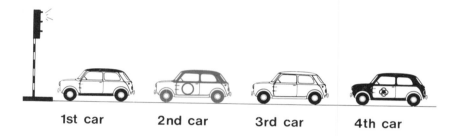

1st car   2nd car   3rd car   4th car

(ii) The six words forming the sentence:

"Division by zero is not defined"

taken in the order in which they occur:

division, by, zero, is, not, defined.

(iii) The ten numbers from 1 to 10 taken in their natural order:

1, 2, 3, 4, 5, 6, 7, 8, 9, 10

The objects forming the sequence (cars, words or numbers in these examples) are called its elements. For the present we shall consider only finite sequences like those above; that is, sequences comprising a definite number of elements. Infinite sequences will be considered later.

There are several ways of specifying a sequence; the simplest way, used in our examples above, is to list all the elements in order. Sometimes we use an *incomplete list* and indicate by dots that there are missing elements; for example, we could abbreviate the third list to:

1, 2, 3, . . . , 10

Such incomplete lists should be used only in cases where the context makes it clear what the missing elements are.

The notation used for listing sequences is similar to the notation for sets, but we distinguish sequences from sets by enclosing the lists in braces in the case of a set only. This notational distinction is necessary because of the distinction between the concepts of a sequence and a set, which is that the order of the elements matters in a sequence but not in a set.

Re-arranging the elements in a sequence gives a new sequence, but re-arranging the elements in a set gives the same set. For example, the sequence 1, 2, 3 is distinct from the sequence 3, 1, 2 but

$$\{1, 2, 3\} = \{3, 1, 2\}$$

However, it may not always be practicable to describe a sequence by means of a complete or incomplete list. For example, if a sequence has a million elements, then a complete list of them may occupy a thousand pages, and an incomplete list may not give enough information to specify the sequence unambiguously. In such cases it may be possible to describe the sequence economically by giving a rule or formula for determining which object appears in each position of the sequence. (In fact, some sequences occur naturally this way, as we shall see.) In the language of *Unit 1, Functions*, we specify the sequence by defining a function. The domain of this function will comprise the first N natural numbers, i.e. be the set $\{1, 2, 3, \ldots, N\}$, where N is the number of elements in the sequence; the rule must be one from which, given any natural number k belonging to the domain, we can determine the kth member of the sequence. As a simple example, the sequence comprising the reciprocals of the first million natural numbers is specified by the function, f say, with rule

$k \longmapsto \dfrac{1}{k}$ and domain $\{1, 2, \ldots, 1\,000\,000\}$.

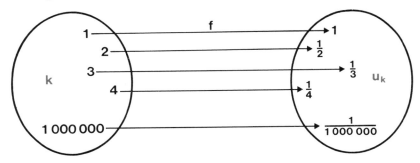

We may specify f by means of the formula

$$f : k \longmapsto \frac{1}{k} \qquad (k \in \{1, 2, \ldots, 1\,000\,000\})$$

or

$$f(k) = \frac{1}{k} \qquad (k \in \{1, 2, \ldots, 1\,000\,000\})$$

Either of these formulas tells us that, for every integer k between 1 and $1\,000\,000$, the kth term of the sequence, denoted by $f(k)$, is equal to $\dfrac{1}{k}$.

As a further abbreviation, it is customary to follow the conventions of *Unit 4, Finite Differences*, and write u_k (or some other letter with a subscript k) rather than $f(k)$ for the kth element of the sequence. It is also customary to abbreviate the description of the domain slightly, so that the above example would usually be shortened to

$$u_k = \frac{1}{k} \qquad (k = 1, 2, \ldots, 1\,000\,000)$$

Exercise 1

Write the sequence specified by

$$u_n = n(n + 1) \quad (n = 1, 2, \ldots, 5)$$

as a complete list.

Exercise 1
(2 minutes)

■

4

Exercise 2

Fill in the boxes so that the formula

$$u_r = \boxed{} \quad \left(r = \boxed{}\right)$$

specifies the sequence $\frac{1}{2}$, 1, 2, 4, 8, 16, 32.

7.1.2   The Use of Sequences in Computing

7.1.2

In *Unit 2, Errors and Accuracy*, we described the iterative method for approximately solving equations of the form

Discussion

$$f(x) = 0$$

Equation (1)

The idea of this method is to start with a guess at the solution and systematically refine it, by repetitions of a fairly simple procedure, until the required accuracy has been reached. Let us denote by u_k the best available approximation to the solution before the kth application of the refinement procedure, and denote by N the total number of applications of this procedure; then the numbers $u_1, u_2, \ldots, u_{N+1}$ form a sequence whose elements are successively better approximations to the solution of Equation (1). Such a sequence is called a sequence of successive approximations to the solution of the equation. Here we study them not only for their utility but also because they form a natural introduction to the idea of a limit.

Definition 1
* * *

In many successive approximation methods, the procedure for calculating a new approximation, say u_k, requires a knowledge of the previous approximation u_{k-1}, but not of any of the earlier approximations. An example is the method for approximately solving a cubic equation, described in the television component of this unit, where each new approximation to the solution can be calculated from the previous one by means of the formula:

$$u_1 = \text{initial guess at the solution}$$

$$u_k = \tfrac{1}{5}(u_{k-1}^3 + 3)$$

Another example is Newton's method for evaluating square roots. If a is a number whose square root is required, and u_{k-1} is an approximation to $\sqrt{a}$, then Newton's method is to take as the next approximation the number

Definition 2

$$u_k = \frac{1}{2}\left(u_{k-1} + \frac{a}{u_{k-1}}\right)$$

Equation (2)

That is, the arithmetic mean (the average) of u_{k-1} and $\dfrac{a}{u_{k-1}}$ is used as an approximation to their geometric mean (the square root of their product), which is precisely $\sqrt{a}$.

As an illustration of Newton's method, here is a calculation of $\sqrt{10}$ to

(continued on page 6)

Solution 7.1.1.1

Solution 7.1.1.1

    2, 6, 12, 20, 30   ■

Solution 7.1.1.2

Solution 7.1.1.2

$$u_r = \boxed{2^{r-2}} \quad \left(r = \boxed{1, 2, \ldots, 7}\right)$$ ■

(continued from page 5)

3 places of decimals, starting from 3 as a first crude approximation to the value of $\sqrt{10}$:

$$u_1 = 3 \qquad \text{(first estimate)}$$

$$u_2 = \frac{1}{2}\left(3 + \frac{10}{3}\right) = 3.167 \text{ to 3 decimals} \quad (k = 2)$$

$$u_3 = \frac{1}{2}\left(3.167 + \frac{10}{3.167}\right) = 3.162 \qquad (k = 3)$$

$$u_4 = \frac{1}{2}\left(3.162 + \frac{10}{3.162}\right) = 3.162 \qquad (k = 4)$$

If we calculated more approximations, starting with u_5, we would just be repeating the calculation that led to this 3-decimal-place approximation to u_4, and we would get the same number 3.162 again. Thus the method gives 3.162 as the value of $\sqrt{10}$ to 3 decimal places. One way to make sure that this number really is $\sqrt{10}$ to this degree of accuracy is to square it. We get

$$(3.162)^2 = 9.998$$

and since

$$(3.163)^2 = 10.005$$

the number 3.162 is indeed the best approximation to $\sqrt{10}$ with only 3 decimal places.

Exercise 1

Exercise 1
(4 minutes)

Use Newton's square-root process to calculate $\sqrt{2}$ to three places of decimals, using 1 as your first approximation. It is convenient in this case to write Equation (2) (with $a = 2$) in the form:

$$u_k = \frac{1}{2}u_{k-1} + \frac{1}{u_{k-1}}$$

Part of a table of reciprocals, with provision for linear interpolation, is given at the right for your convenience. The blank table below is for your results.

x	$\dfrac{1}{x}$	differences
1.40	0.714	
1.41	0.709	-5
1.42	0.704	-5

k	$\frac{1}{2}u_{k-1}$	$\dfrac{1}{u_{k-1}}$	u_k

■

A formula such as Equation (2), expressing each element in a sequence (except the first) in terms of its predecessors, is called a recurrence formula. The most general recurrence formula would have the form

Main Text
* * *
Definition 3
* * *

$$u_k = F(u_{k-1}, u_{k-2}, u_{k-3}, \ldots)$$

where F is some function. In this unit we shall only consider the simplest type of recurrence formula, in which each element depends only on its immediate predecessor. A general recurrence formula of this type is

$$u_k = F(u_{k-1})$$

where F is some function. The calculation implied by this formula can be represented by a diagram:

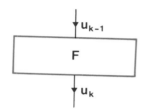

indicating that we put the number u_{k-1} into the function F and get out of it the number u_k.

Since k can have any of the values $2, 3, \ldots, N$, where N is the number of elements in the sequence, the above diagram really stands for $(N-1)$ different diagrams in which k takes these different values. These $(N-1)$ diagrams can be joined up to give a new diagram representing the entire process by which we compute the successive elements of the sequence $u_1, u_2, \ldots, u_N$.

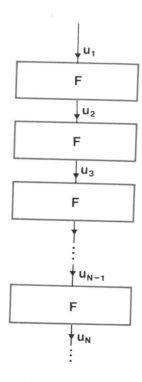

A computer programmer would represent this process by a more compact diagram which emphasizes the fact that the same function F is used repeatedly and the refinement calculation need therefore be programmed

(continued on page 9)

Solution 1 **Solution 1**

k	$\frac{1}{2}u_{k-1}$	$\dfrac{1}{u_{k-1}}$	u_k
1	—	—	1
2	0.5	1	1.5
3	0.75	0.667	1.417
4	0.708	0.706	1.414
5	0.707	0.707	1.414

When the given formula is used with $u_1 = 1$, we find

$$u_2 = 0.5 + 1$$
$$= 1.5$$

and

$$u_3 = 0.75 + 0.667$$
$$= 1.417$$

The formula now requires us to find $\dfrac{1}{1.417}$, and we are given tabulated values of the reciprocal for $\dfrac{1}{1.41}$ and $\dfrac{1}{1.42}$ but not for any of the points in between. We can, however, use linear interpolation to get a value for $\dfrac{1}{1.417}$. This gives

$$\frac{1}{1.417} = 0.709 - 0.005 \times \frac{7}{10}$$
$$= 0.7055$$

Then the formula gives

$$u_4 = 0.7085 + 0.7055$$
$$= 1.414$$

Using linear interpolation again we find

$$u_5 = 0.707 + 0.709 - 0.002$$
$$= 1.414$$

Further iterations would just repeat the calculation that gave u_5, and so we can stop the process here, giving the result as

$$\sqrt{2} = 1.414 \text{ (to 3 decimal places).} \qquad \blacksquare$$

(continued from page 7)

only once. The essential new feature of this diagram would be the replacement of the chain in the second diagram by the loop:

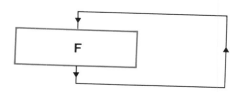

Here the upward arrow at the right indicates that the "output" of each application of the function F (except the last) is used as the "input" for the next application.

Exercise 2

Exercise 2
(2 minutes)

If a sequence of at least ten elements has the recurrence formula

$$u_k = F(u_{k-1})$$

where F is some function with domain R and codomain R, show that

$$u_3 = F \circ F(u_1)$$

(The circle denotes composition of functions as in section 1.2.2 of *Unit 1, Functions*.) Write down corresponding formulas giving

(i) u_4 in terms of u_1
(ii) u_{10} in terms of u_8. ∎

Exercise 3

Exercise 3
(2 minutes)

A savings bank offers the rate of interest $r\%$ compounded annually. A man deposits some money and leaves it for several years. If the amount of money to his credit after k years is £u_k, write down a recurrence formula for the sequence $u_1, u_2, \ldots$. (Assume that this bank works with exact arithmetic instead of approximating by whole-penny amounts as real banks do.) ∎

7.1.3 Summary

7.1.3

Summary

In this section we have defined a finite sequence and given some examples which illustrate the following three ways in which a finite sequence may be specified:

(i) by giving a complete or incomplete list of its elements;
(ii) by defining a function, f, with domain $\{1, 2, \ldots, N\}$ such that the kth element of the sequence is $f(k)$ where $k = 1, 2, \ldots, N$;
(iii) by giving the first term in the sequence, u_1, together with a recurrence formula, $u_k = F(u_{k-1})$, which specifies the kth element of the sequence, u_k, as the image of its predecessor, u_{k-1}, under the function F.

An important type of finite sequence is a sequence of successive approximations to the solution of an equation, which may conveniently be specified in way (iii) above, where u_1 is a rough guess at the solution, and the function F is used to refine the approximate solution u_{k-1} to u_k. The calculation of the solution can easily be programmed for a computer as the same refinement algorithm is used at each step.

Solution 7.1.2.2

Since the codomain of F is the same as the domain of F, the composition $F \circ F$ is properly defined. (See Exercise 1.2.2.2(i) of *Unit 1, Functions.*)
So the answers are

(i) $u_4 = F(u_3) = F(F(u_2)) = F(F(F(u_1)))$
$= F \circ F \circ F(u_1)$

(ii) $u_{10} = F \circ F(u_8).$ ∎

Solution 7.1.2.3

At the beginning of the kth year the account contains $£u_{k-1}$. The amount of interest credited during the year is $\dfrac{r}{100}u_{k-1}$, and so the balance at the end of the kth year is $u_{k-1} + \dfrac{r}{100}u_{k-1}$. Accordingly the recurrence relation is

$$u_k = \left(1 + \frac{r}{100}\right)u_{k-1}$$

We shall look at this sort of relation again later in this text when we discuss the exponential function. ∎

7.2 INFINITE SEQUENCES

7.2.0 Introduction

In the previous section we restricted our discussion to finite sequences, i.e. sequences with a finite number of elements. Thus a finite sequence can be specified by a function $k \longmapsto u_k$ with domain $\{1, 2, \ldots, N\}$. On the other hand a sequence specified by a function $k \longmapsto u_k$ with domain Z^+, the set of *all* positive integers, is called an infinite sequence.

The fundamental concept in the theory of infinite sequences is the concept of a *limit*. Roughly speaking, if a sequence consists of successive approximations to some number, then that number is called the limit of the sequence. This definition is too imprecise, however, to serve as the foundation for a mathematical theory. In mathematics, although we can choose whatever meanings we like for the technical terms and concepts we work with, we must always make these meanings precise and unambiguous. Our next object of study will therefore be the notion of a limit of an infinite sequence.

7.2.1 The Specification of Infinite Sequences

To be able to discuss infinite sequences we must first be able to specify them. The methods used are just the same as for finite sequences except that a complete list is never possible. Here is an example where the same sequence is specified by the three different methods:

(i) incomplete list

$1, 2, 4, 8, 16, 32, \ldots$

(ii) function

$k \longmapsto 2^{k-1} \quad (k \in Z^+)$

(iii) <u>recurrence formula</u>

$$u_1 = 1$$

$$u_k = 2u_{k-1} \quad (k = 2, 3, \dots)$$

A good way of getting an idea of the behaviour of a sequence quickly is to draw the graph of its function. Here is the graph representing the infinite sequence

$$0.3, 0.33, 0.333, 0.3333, \dots$$

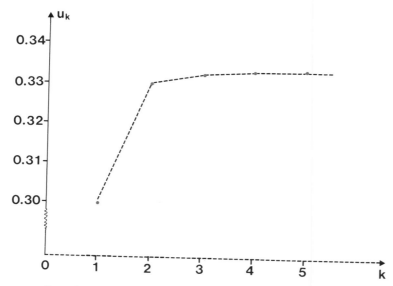

**Graph of the sequence 0.3, 0.33, 0.333, 0.3333, ...
The dashed lines are to guide the eye only ;
they are not part of the graph.**

Exercise 1

List the first 5 elements of the sequences specified by :

(i) $u_n = (-1)^n \qquad (n \in Z^+)$

(ii) $u_1 = 3$

$$u_k = 3 + \frac{u_{k-1}}{10} \quad (k = 2, 3, 4, \dots)$$ ■

Exercise 1
(2 minutes)

Exercise 2

Write down functions that specify the following sequences :

(i) $1, -2, 3, -4, 5, -6, \dots$

(ii) $u_1 = 0$

$$u_k = \frac{1}{2 - u_{k-1}} \quad (k = 2, 3, 4, \dots)$$ ■

Exercise 2
(2 minutes)

Exercise 3

Write down specifications in terms of recurrence formulas for the sequences :

(i) $1, -1, 1, -1, \dots$

(ii) $u_k = \frac{1}{(-2)^k} \quad (k \in Z^+)$ ■

Exercise 3
(3 minutes)

Solution 1

(i) $-1, 1, -1, 1, -1$

(ii) $3, 3.3, 3.33, 3.333, 3.3333$ ■

Solution 2

(i) $k \longmapsto k \cdot (-1)^{k+1}$ $(k \in Z^+)$

(ii) The sequence is

$$0, \tfrac{1}{2}, \tfrac{2}{3}, \tfrac{3}{4}, \tfrac{4}{5}, \tfrac{5}{6}, \ldots$$

and a function which specifies this sequence is

$$k \longmapsto \frac{k-1}{k} \quad \text{or} \quad k \longmapsto 1 - \frac{1}{k} \quad (k \in Z^+)$$ ■

Solution 3

(i) $u_1 = 1$

   $u_k = -u_{k-1}$ $(k = 2, 3, 4, \ldots)$

(ii) $u_1 = -\tfrac{1}{2}$

   $u_k = -\tfrac{1}{2} u_{k-1}$ $(k = 2, 3, 4, \ldots)$ ■

7.2.2 Limits

In this sub-section we discuss the main topic of this unit: the concept of a *limit*. As with any mathematical concept, there are two ways of looking at it: the intuitive and the rigorous. The intuitive aspect enables us to recognize the situations where the concept is likely to be useful, and the rigorous aspect enables us to apply it correctly. Both are essential to a proper understanding; it is true that many users of mathematics do succeed in getting by on the intuitive aspect alone, but it is rather like travelling in a car without a spare tyre: at any moment a situation may arise with which the available equipment cannot cope. Accordingly we shall consider both aspects of the concept of a limit here. We begin with the intuitive definition and work towards a rigorous definition.

The intuitive notion of a limit has already been mentioned on page 10: if an infinite sequence is a sequence of successive approximations to some number, then we call that number the limit of the sequence. For example, the sequence

$$0.3, 0.33, 0.333, 0.3333, 0.33333, \ldots$$

is a sequence of successively closer decimal approximations to the number $\tfrac{1}{3}$; its limit is therefore $\tfrac{1}{3}$. If we denote the sequence $u_1, u_2, u_3, \ldots$ by u, a convenient formulation of this intuitive notion is

> **Intuitive Definition of a Limit**
>
> "The number $\lim u$ is the limit of the infinite sequence u" is equivalent to the statement "if k is very large, then u_k is a very good approximation to $\lim u$".

A slightly different, but equivalent, definition is used in the television programme.

Not every sequence has a limit; for example neither of the sequences

$$1, 2, 4, 8, 16, \ldots, 2^{k-1}, \ldots \quad \text{and} \quad 1, 0, 1, 0, 1, \ldots$$

has a limit.

In the first sequence the elements increase with k and in the second they oscillate between 0 and 1: in neither case is there a number which satisfies our intuitive definition of a limit. We distinguish two types of sequence: we say that a sequence having a limit is convergent (or that it converges) and that one without a limit is non-convergent. (The term "divergent" is also very common.)

Definition 2
* * *
Definition 3
* * *

To see whether a sequence is convergent or not it is often helpful to look at its graph.* Here are the graphs of the first two sequences given above. Can you see the geometrical property of the first graph that corresponds to the convergent character of the sequence?

Discussion

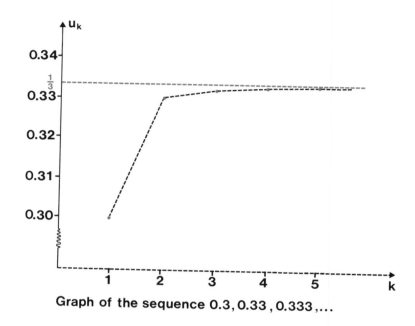

Graph of the sequence 0.3, 0.33, 0.333, ...

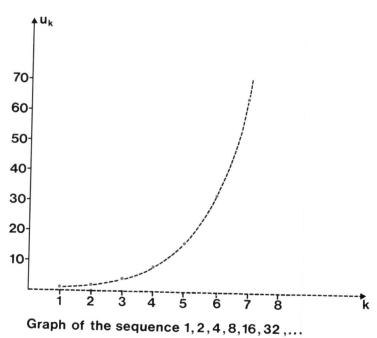

Graph of the sequence 1, 2, 4, 8, 16, 32, ...

* The graph of a sequence u is the graph of the function which defines the sequence, namely the set $\{(k, u_k)\}$.

The first sequence consists of successive approximations to the number $\frac{1}{3}$, and so as k increases the points of the graph get steadily closer to the red line. In the second graph we cannot draw a line with this property. These examples illustrate that the graph of a convergent sequence u is characterized by this property: for large k, the points (k, u_k) are very close to a line parallel to the k-axis and at a distance lim u from it.

Exercise 1

Here are graphs of some infinite sequences. Which are convergent and what are the limits of the convergent ones? ($k \in Z^+$ throughout.)

If in doubt, do not guess: use the criterion given at the end of the preceding paragraph (or, if you prefer, the intuitive definition of a limit given on page 12).

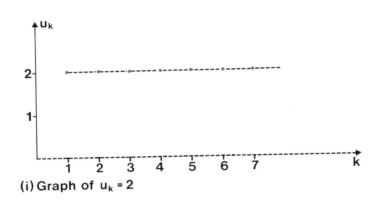

(i) Graph of $u_k = 2$

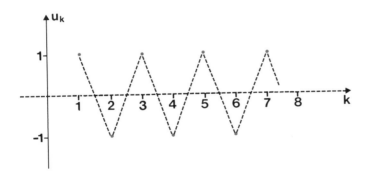

(ii) Graph of $u_k = (-1)^{k+1}$

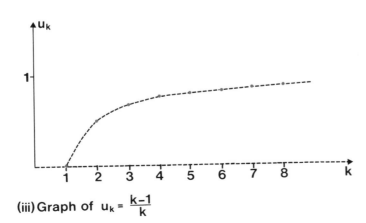

(iii) Graph of $u_k = \dfrac{k-1}{k}$

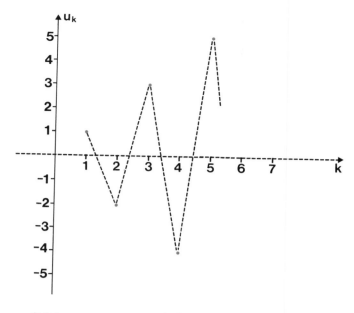

(iv) Graph of $u_k = (-1)^{k-1}k$

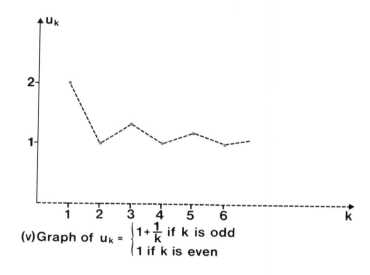

(v) Graph of $u_k = \begin{cases} 1 + \dfrac{1}{k} & \text{if } k \text{ is odd} \\ 1 & \text{if } k \text{ is even} \end{cases}$

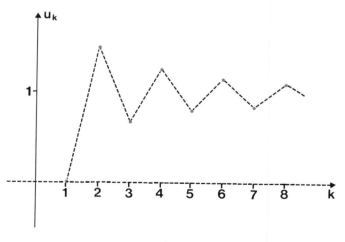

(vi) Graph of $u_k = 1 + \dfrac{(-1)^k}{k}$

(continued on page 16)

Solution 1   **Solution 1**

 (i) Convergent, with limit 2. Here the points (k, u_k) all lie *on* the line parallel to the k-axis at a distance 2 units from it.
 (ii) Not convergent.
(iii) Convergent, with limit 1.
(iv) Not convergent.
 (v) Convergent, with limit 1.
(vi) Convergent, with limit 1.   ∎

(*continued from page 15*)

Exercise 2   **Exercise 2**
                                                                                                               (5 minutes)

Which of the following sequences are convergent, and what are the limits of the convergent ones?

 (i) $u_k = k$

 (ii) $u_k = \dfrac{1}{k}$

(iii) $u_k = \begin{cases} \dfrac{1}{\sqrt{k}} & \text{if } k \text{ is even} \\ 0 & \text{if } k \text{ is odd} \end{cases}$

(iv) $u_k = 1 + \dfrac{1}{k}$

 (v) $u_k = \dfrac{1}{10^6} + \dfrac{1}{k}$

where $k \in Z^+$ in each case.   ∎

This last exercise may give some idea of the difficulties we can get into if   **Discussion**
we "travel without a spare tyre" by relying entirely on the intuitive notion   * *

of a limit. For large k, the elements of the sequence $u_k = \dfrac{1}{10^6} + \dfrac{1}{k}$ in (v)

are all very good approximations to the number $\dfrac{1}{10^6}$, and so $\dfrac{1}{10^6}$ satisfies

the intuitive definition of the limit; but since $\dfrac{1}{10^6}$ is very close to 0, the

elements are also "very good approximations" to 0, so that it would appear that 0 could equally well be called the limit. This shows that the intuitive definition of a limit given on page 12 can lead to ambiguities if it is pushed too far. Some of these are explored in the television programme. Our task now is to find a definition that is free from such ambiguities.

One reason why the intuitive definition of a limit leads to ambiguities is that the phrases "k is very large" and "u_k is a very good approximation to lim u" have not been defined. In fact, these are phrases whose meanings depend on the circumstances: what seems large to a mouse may not seem large to an elephant; to a butcher weighing meat 0.499 kg may seem a good approximation to 0.5 kg but it will not seem so to a pharmacist measuring out a dangerous drug. The problem of making precise statements about approximations was considered in *Unit 2, Errors and Accuracy*, and we saw there that the way to do it was to specify an absolute error bound. Thus if we denote this absolute error bound, which is a positive number, by ε (the Greek letter called "epsilon"), then we can interpret the statement "u_k is a very good approximation to lim u" to mean that the difference between u_k and lim u is less than or equal to the absolute error bound, ε. In symbols, this can be written

$$|u_k - \lim u| \leqslant \varepsilon$$

or equivalently

$$-\varepsilon \leqslant u_k - \lim u \leqslant \varepsilon$$

Another way of writing the same condition, obtained by adding $\lim u$ to all members of the inequalities, is

$$\lim u - \varepsilon \leqslant u_k \leqslant \lim u + \varepsilon$$

which is the same as

$$u_k \in [\lim u - \varepsilon, \lim u + \varepsilon]$$

where

$$[\lim u - \varepsilon, \lim u + \varepsilon]$$

(defined on page 24 of *Unit 1, Functions*) stands for the set of all real numbers x satisfying

$$\lim u - \varepsilon \leqslant x \leqslant \lim u + \varepsilon$$

We call this set the error interval associated with the limit $\lim u$ and the absolute error bound ε. (Thus if the limit is 1 and the error bound is 0.005, then the error interval comprises all real numbers from 0.995 to 1.005 inclusive.)

The vital question now is "How accurate is very accurate?" or, in other words: "How small is ε?" Remembering the sequence

$$u_k = \frac{1}{10^6} + \frac{1}{k} \quad (k \in Z^+)$$

and our subsequent discussion on page 16, we would have to have $\varepsilon < \frac{1}{10^6}$ in order to decide whether $\frac{1}{10^6}$ or 0 is the limit of this sequence.

But if we take $\varepsilon = \frac{1}{10^8}$ say, then we still cannot decide between $\frac{1}{10^6}$ and $\frac{1001}{10^9}$. In fact, whatever value we choose for ε, there are still a lot of possible values for $\lim u$ within the error interval defined by $\frac{1}{10^6}$ and ε. And yet, intuitively, the sequence converges to $\frac{1}{10^6}$. So we drop the idea of one ε and say that the sequence u has limit $\lim u$ if for *any* positive value of ε, u_k lies within the error interval $[\lim u - \varepsilon, \lim u + \varepsilon]$ when k is very large. This means that we can now choose between $\frac{1}{10^6}$ and $\frac{1001}{10^9}$, say, as the limit of our sequence, because we can take ε smaller than $\frac{1}{10^6} - \frac{1001}{10^9}$. In general, we can distinguish between $\frac{1}{10^6}$ and any other suggested value for $\lim u$.

We now want to frame a definition for "k is very large" that gives a similar precision to this statement. To see how this can be done, look at the following diagrams, where the graph of the sequence

$$u_k = 1 + \frac{(-1)^k 4}{(k + 2)^2} \quad (k \in Z^+)$$

is plotted. A similar diagram is used in the television component of this unit.

(*continued on page 18*)

Solution 2

The quickest way to do these is by using the Intuitive Definition on page 12, but if you are unsure of how to use it, draw the graphs as well.

(i) Divergent. The elements increase with k; they never get close together, as they would if the sequence converged.

(ii) Convergent with limit 0. The elements get closer and closer to 0 as k increases.

(iii) Convergent with limit 0. Half the members of the sequence are actually equal to 0, and the other members get closer and closer to 0 as k increases.

(iv) Convergent with limit 1. Since $\frac{1}{k}$ is very small for large k, the quantity $1 + \frac{1}{k}$ is very close to 1 when k is large.

(v) Convergent with limit $\frac{1}{10^6}$. See the discussion on page 16. ■

(continued from page 17)

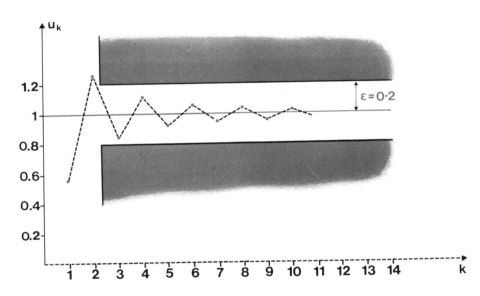

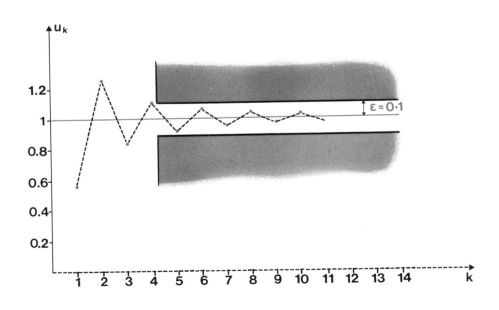

In the first diagram the only points of the graph that do not lie between the parallel lines representing the error interval $[1 - 0.2, 1 + 0.2]$ are those with $k = 1$ and $k = 2$; consequently, with $\varepsilon = 0.2$, we can say that the "very large" values of k start at 3. In the second diagram the only points which are not between the parallel lines representing the error interval $[1 - 0.1, 1 + 0.1]$ are the ones with $k = 1, 2, 3$ and 4; consequently, with $\varepsilon = 0.1$, the "very large" values of k start at 5. If ε is made smaller, more and more k values get left outside the parallel lines, but it is always possible to pick a point on the graph (like the point $(3, u_3)$ for $\varepsilon = 0.2$ or $(5, u_5)$ for $\varepsilon = 0.1$) to the right of which *all* the points of the graph lie between the parallel lines. This is the essential part: for *any* positive value of the absolute error bound ε, there is an element of the sequence after which all the elements lie in the error interval

$$[1 - \varepsilon, 1 + \varepsilon]$$

For example, if ε is $\dfrac{1}{10^6}$, then the condition for an element u_k to lie in the error interval is

$$1 - \frac{1}{10^6} \leqslant 1 + \frac{(-1)^k 4}{(2 + k)^2} \leqslant 1 + \frac{1}{10^6}$$

By the rules for manipulating inequalities (see *Unit 6, Inequalities*), we can subtract 1 from every member of these inequalities, obtaining

$$-\frac{1}{10^6} \leqslant \frac{(-1)^k 4}{(2 + k)^2} \leqslant \frac{1}{10^6}$$

Since $(-1)^k$ take the values $+1$ and -1 only, this pair of inequalities is satisfied if

$$-\frac{1}{10^6} \leqslant \frac{-4}{(2 + k)^2} \quad \text{and} \quad \frac{4}{(2 + k)^2} \leqslant \frac{1}{10^6}$$

Since these last two inequalities are equivalent, it is sufficient to require

$$\frac{4}{(2 + k)^2} \leqslant \frac{1}{10^6}$$

which is equivalent to $4\,000\,000 \leqslant (2 + k)^2$, and is therefore true for all $k \geqslant 1998$. If ε is $\dfrac{1}{10^6}$, then all elements after the 1998th lie in the error interval.

Generalizing this idea to any infinite sequence, we can now adopt the following definition:

Main Text
* * *

Definition 4
* * *

> ### Rigorous Definition of a Limit
>
> "The number $\lim u$ is the limit of the infinite sequence u" is equivalent to the statement "for any positive error bound ε, there is an element of the sequence after which every element lies within the error interval $[\lim u - \varepsilon, \lim u + \varepsilon]$."

In effect, this definition states that, whatever accuracy we choose to work with, we can always use $u_1, u_2, u_3, \ldots$ as a sequence of successive approximations for calculating the number $\lim u$ (if $\lim u$ exists); for there is an element in the sequence beyond which all the elements are (to this accuracy) indistinguishable from each other, and so any of these elements may be used as the calculated approximate value of $\lim u$.

(In the television programme, Definition 4 is given in a slightly different, but equivalent, form.)

It takes quite a lot of experience to get used to Definition 4. If you are unhappy about it, look again at the two diagrams on page 18 and try to imagine how they would look if ε were still further reduced, and whether a suitable value of N (the distance from the u_k-axis to the shaded area) could be found however small ε were chosen. In doing this, remember that the graph we have drawn only shows the first few elements in the sequence, but that the true graph extends indefinitely to the right, since the sequence has no last element. (Indeed, the concepts of a limit and of convergence do not apply to finite sequences.)

One of the difficulties in using the rigorous definition of a limit is that it requires us to prove something about *any* positive value of ε, and about *every* element after the Nth in the sequence. We cannot deal individually with each value of ε or every element of the sequence; so instead we must find a way of dealing with them all at once. In effect we have to prove a tiny theorem for each individual sequence. The following example shows how it is done.

Example 1

Example 1

Show that 0 is the limit of the sequence $1, \frac{1}{2}, \frac{1}{3} \ldots$.

The definition requires us to show that for any positive error bound ε there is an element (say the Nth) after which all elements are within the error interval $[0 - \varepsilon, 0 + \varepsilon]$. As a start, let us show it for a particular value of ε, say $\frac{1}{10}$. Then, since the kth element of the sequence is $\frac{1}{k}$, it is a question of finding a positive integer N such that all elements u_k after the Nth satisfy

$$-\frac{1}{10} \leqslant u_k \leqslant \frac{1}{10}$$

That is, we wish to find $N \in Z^+$ such that

$$-\frac{1}{10} \leqslant \frac{1}{k} \leqslant \frac{1}{10} \quad (k \in Z^+ \text{ and } k > N)$$

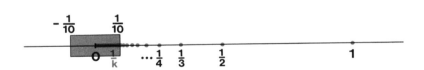

Now the inequality $-\frac{1}{10} \leqslant \frac{1}{k}$ is satisfied for all $k \in Z^+$, so that it implies no restriction on N.

To deal with the inequality $\frac{1}{k} \leqslant \frac{1}{10}$ we find its solution set using the methods of *Unit 6, Inequalities*. Multiplying both sides of the inequality by $10k$, (a step that is justified since $k \in Z^+$), we find that it is equivalent to

$$10 \leqslant k \quad (k \in Z^+ \text{ and } k > N)$$

That is, we want to find a positive integer N such that every integer k greater than N is also greater than or equal to 10. There are many numbers N with this property; one of them is 10 itself. So we have shown that if ε has the particular value $\frac{1}{10}$ we can satisfy the definition of a limit for this sequence by taking $N = 10$.

To complete the proof that 0 is the limit of the sequence $u_k = \dfrac{1}{k}$ we must show that for *any* positive ε, not necessarily $\frac{1}{10}$, we can find an N that satisfies the definition. That is, we must find a positive integer N such that

$$-\varepsilon \leqslant \frac{1}{k} \leqslant \varepsilon \quad (k \in Z^+ \text{ and } k > N)$$

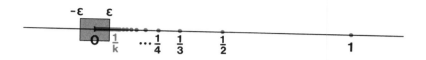

Once again the inequality $-\varepsilon \leqslant \dfrac{1}{k}$ places no restriction on N. The inequality $\dfrac{1}{k} \leqslant \varepsilon$ is equivalent to

$$k \geqslant \frac{1}{\varepsilon} \qquad (k \in Z^+ \text{ and } k > N)$$

and so we want an integer N such that every integer k greater than N is also greater than $\dfrac{1}{\varepsilon}$ (which must be positive, but need not be an integer).

Such an N can indeed be found; for example, the first integer after $\dfrac{1}{\varepsilon}$ will do. Since we can find a suitable N for *any positive ε, however small,* the definition of a limit is satisfied, and so 0 is proved to be the limit of the sequence $u_k = \dfrac{1}{k}$. ■

Exercise 3

Exercise 3
(4 minutes)

Verify, using Definition 4, that the limit of the sequence $u_k = \dfrac{1}{k^2}$ is 0.

You can take N to be the first integer after the number $\dfrac{1}{\sqrt{\varepsilon}}$. ■

Exercise 4

Exercise 4
(5 minutes)

Verify, using Definition 4, that the limit of the sequence 0.3, 0.33, 0.333, 0.3333,... is $\frac{1}{3}$. You can use the fact that

$$\frac{1}{3} - \underbrace{0.33\ldots3}_{k\,\text{digits}} = \underbrace{0.00\ldots0}_{k\,\text{zeros}}333\ldots = \frac{1}{3} \times 10^{-k}$$

and, for any particular ε, take N to be the number of consecutive zeros after the decimal point in the decimal representation of ε. ■

Solution 3

We want to show that for any positive ε there exists a positive integer N such that

$$-\varepsilon \leqslant \frac{1}{k^2} - 0 \leqslant \varepsilon \quad (k \in Z^+ \text{ and } k > N)$$

The left-hand inequality places no restriction on N. The right-hand inequality is equivalent (since ε and k^2 are positive) to

$$\frac{1}{\varepsilon} \leqslant k^2$$

and hence to

$$\frac{1}{\sqrt{\varepsilon}} \leqslant k$$

For the definition of a limit to be satisfied therefore, we want an N large enough to ensure that, whenever k is greater than N, then it is greater than or equal to $\dfrac{1}{\sqrt{\varepsilon}}$. The value of N suggested in the question is large enough for this purpose. ∎

Solution 4

We want to show that, for any positive ε, there is a positive integer N such that

$$\tfrac{1}{3} - \varepsilon \leqslant 0.\underbrace{333\ldots3}_{k \text{ digits}} \leqslant \tfrac{1}{3} + \varepsilon \quad (k \in Z^+ \text{ and } k > N)$$

The right-hand inequality places no restriction on N, since

$$0.\underbrace{33\ldots3}_{k \text{ digits}} \leqslant \tfrac{1}{3} \leqslant \tfrac{1}{3} + \varepsilon$$

for all allowed values of k and ε. The left-hand inequality can be written

$$\tfrac{1}{3} - \varepsilon \leqslant \tfrac{1}{3} - 0.\underbrace{00\ldots0}_{k \text{ zeros}}333\ldots$$

which is equivalent to

$$0.\underbrace{00\ldots0}_{k \text{ zeros}}33\ldots \leqslant \varepsilon \quad (k \in Z^+ \text{ and } k > N)$$

We want to find an N that is large enough to ensure that if $k > N$ then the above inequality is satisfied. The suggestion in the question is to choose N so as to give ε a decimal representation of the form

$$\varepsilon = 0.\underbrace{00\ldots0}_{N \text{ zeros}}a_1 a_2 \ldots$$

with $a_1 \geqslant 1$.

Then if $k > N$, the decimal representation of $\tfrac{1}{3} - u_k$ has more consecutive zeros after the decimal point than that of ε, so that

$$0.\underbrace{00\ldots0}_{k \text{ zeros}}33\ldots \leqslant 0.\underbrace{00\ldots0}_{N \text{ zeros}}a_1 a_2 \ldots$$

is indeed satisfied. Thus we have verified that for any ε there does exist an element u_N beyond which all elements are in $[\tfrac{1}{3} - \varepsilon, \tfrac{1}{3} + \varepsilon]$, and so by the definition of a limit the sequence has limit $\tfrac{1}{3}$. ∎

7.2.3 Limits of Real Functions

Although the notion of a limit takes its simplest form when applied to sequences, it is by no means restricted to sequences in its application. For example, when a bell is struck, the pressure in the air nearby will vary with time roughly as shown below.

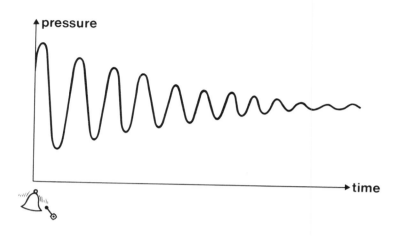

The amplitude of the oscillations decreases slowly with time, so that a long time after the bell is struck the pressure is approximately constant and equal to the atmospheric pressure.

This graph is qualitatively similar to the graph of a convergent sequence, for example part (vi) of Exercise 7.2.2.1 (page 15), and so we may expect to be able to use the ideas of convergence and of limits here too. In both cases we are dealing with a function: in the bell example because the air pressure depends on the time elapsed since the bell was struck, and in the sequence example because the kth term of the sequence depends on k. The main difference between these two functions is that in the bell example the domain is R^+ whereas for an infinite sequence the domain is Z^+. Despite this difference, both the intuitive and the rigorous definitions of a limit can be carried over quite easily from the case of sequences to the case of functions with domain R^+ (or, in general R).* As another example, here is a graph showing the dependence of atmospheric pressure (at some particular instant of time) on height above the earth's surface.

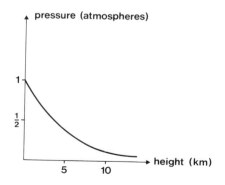

When the height is very large, the atmospheric pressure is very small.

The similarity of this statement to the Intuitive Definition of a limit of

---

* We remind you that we use the term *real function* for a function whose domain and codomain are R or subsets of R.

an infinite sequence (page 12) suggests that the concept of a limit will also be useful here. Accordingly we adopt the following:

Intuitive
Definition 1
* * *

Intuitive Definition of a Limit

If f is a real function and L is a number, then "L is the limit of f for large numbers in its domain" is equivalent to the statement "whenever x is very large, $f(x)$ is a very good approximation to L".

We use the notation $\lim\limits_{x \text{ large}} f(x)$ for the limit of f for large numbers in its domain.* Thus, if f is the function mapping elapsed time to pressure in the first graph in this section, then $\lim\limits_{x \text{ large}} f(x)$ is the mean atmospheric pressure; and if g is the function mapping height to pressure in the second graph, then $\lim\limits_{x \text{ large}} g(x)$ is 0. The same notation can also be used for limits of sequences; thus the limit of the sequence $1, \frac{1}{2}, \frac{1}{3}, \ldots$ may be written $\lim\limits_{k \text{ large}} \frac{1}{k}$.

Exercise 1

Exercise 1
(2 minutes)

The following functions all have domain R^+. Which ones have a limit for large numbers in their domain, and what are the limits?

(i) $t \longmapsto 4$

(ii) $t \longmapsto t^2$

(iii) $t \longmapsto \dfrac{1}{t}$

(iv) $t \longmapsto \sin t$

(v) $t \longmapsto \dfrac{\sin t}{t}$ ∎

Exercise 2

Exercise 2
(3 minutes)

Write down a precise definition, analogous to Definition 4 on page 19, for the statement $L = \lim\limits_{x \text{ large}} f(x)$, where f is a function with domain R^+. ∎

Discussion

There is another way of applying the concept of a limit to functions. This time the analogy with limits of sequences, though still present, is not quite as close. The need for this new type of limit was foreshadowed in the Introduction to this text, where we mentioned the problem of defining instantaneous velocity. There we considered a car travelling along a straight road, and denoted its distance from the starting point at a time t after starting by $f(t)$. We found that the average velocity over the time interval beginning at some time t_1 and ending at some other time t_2 was given by the formula

$$\text{average velocity in } [t_1, t_2] = \frac{f(t_2) - f(t_1)}{t_2 - t_1}$$

$$= w(t_1, t_2), \text{ say}$$

This formula defines $w(t_1, t_2)$ for $t_1 < t_2$, and also for $t_1 > t_2$, but not for $t_1 = t_2$, because there is no mathematically consistent way of defining division by 0.

---

*Any letter could be used here in place of x, e.g. $\lim\limits_{t \text{ large}} f(t)$. Notations such as $\lim\limits_{x \to \infty} f(x)$ are very commonly used to mean exactly the same thing, but we prefer to avoid the symbol ∞ at this stage, because it is dangerous unless fully understood.

Thus the formula gives the average velocity over any non-vanishing time interval, but does not directly define an instantaneous velocity. We can, however, construct a definition of instantaneous velocity in terms of the average velocities, if we make use of the concept of a limit. It is reasonable to assume that the instantaneous velocity does not change very rapidly or fluctuate wildly, and hence that the average velocity, over a very short time interval which includes the instant t_1, will be a very good approximation to the instantaneous velocity. For simplicity, let us look for a definition of the instantaneous velocity, v_1, at a particular instant, t_1, in terms of the average velocities over time intervals beginning or ending at t_1.

In other words, if we define a function g by:

$$g : t \longmapsto w(t_1, t) \quad (t \in \text{domain of } f \text{ and } t \neq t_1)$$

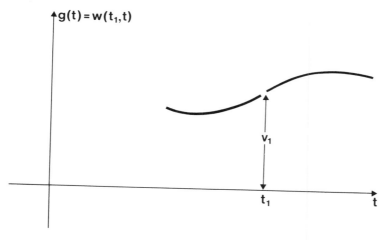

then $g(t)$ is a very good approximation to v_1 whenever t is very close to t_1, but $g(t_1)$ does not exist. This is just like the Intuitive Definition 1 on page 24 for the limit of a function for very large values in its domain, except that here we are concerned with values very close to t_1 instead of very large values. We have thus arrived at a new type of limit, whose intuitive definition may be stated as follows:

Intuitive Definition of a Limit

If g is a real function and a and L are real numbers, "L is the limit of g near a" is equivalent to the statement "if x is very close to a, but not equal to it, then $g(x)$ is very close to L".

Intuitive
Definition 2
* * *

The notation we shall use for the limit of g near a is

$$\lim_{x \to a} g(x)$$

Notation 1
* * *

The notation

$$\lim_{x \to a} g(x)$$

is more common but we are already using the straight arrow for mappings. The limit of g near a is often described as "the limit of $g(x)$ as x approaches (or tends to) a" since it is often convenient to think of the limit in terms of motion: if the value of x changes with time, moving steadily towards a (without ever actually getting there), the value of $g(x)$ changes steadily and eventually gets as close as we please to $\lim_{x \to a} g(x)$. (This is analogous to a way of thinking about limits of sequences which we use in the television programme: if $u_1, u_2, \ldots$ is a convergent infinite sequence and we steadily increase the value of k, then u_k will eventually get as close as we please to the limit of that sequence.)

(continued on page 26)

Solution 1

(i) 4.

(ii) No limit.

(iii) 0; for if ε is any given positive number, then for all $t > \dfrac{1}{\varepsilon}$, $\dfrac{1}{t}$ lies in the error interval $[0 - \varepsilon, 0 + \varepsilon]$.

(iv) No limit.

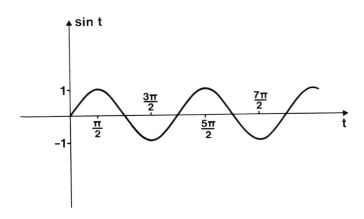

The graph continues to oscillate between 1 and -1 and thus, as with the sequence $1, -1, 1, -1, \ldots$ there is no limit.

(v) 0. Given any positive error bound ε, we can ensure that the value of $\dfrac{\sin t}{t}$ lies in the interval $[-\varepsilon, \varepsilon]$ by choosing $t > \dfrac{1}{\varepsilon}$; for then we have $\left| \dfrac{\sin t}{t} \right| \leqslant \varepsilon$, since $|\sin t| \leqslant 1$. (The argument is similar to the one used in (iii) above.) ∎

Solution 2

We say the number L is the limit of the function f with domain R^+ if, for every positive number ε, there is a number T such that, for all $t > T$,

$$f(t) \in [L - \varepsilon, L + \varepsilon]$$

i.e.

$$L - \varepsilon \leqslant f(t) \leqslant L + \varepsilon$$ ∎

Rigorous
Definition 1
* * *

(continued from page 25)

In this definition you should notice that a itself does not have to belong to the domain of g: the definition is concerned with values of x that are very close to a, but not with $x = a$. If a does belong to the domain of g, the value of $g(a)$ does not affect the value of $\lim\limits_{x \to a} g(x)$ and the two numbers may be either the same or different. If a does not belong to the domain of g then $g(a)$ does not exist, but even so $\lim\limits_{x \to a} g(x)$ may still exist. In the following example the limits for x near 1 and -1 have just the same values as if the graph were an unbroken straight line:

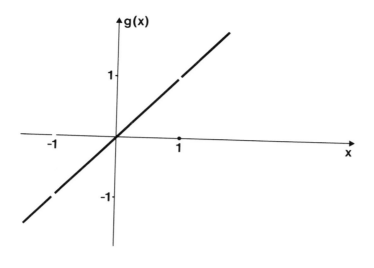

The above diagram is a graph of the function g defined by

$$g : x \longmapsto \begin{cases} x & \text{if } x \neq 1 \\ 0 & \text{if } x = 1 \end{cases} \quad (x \in R \text{ and } x \neq -1)$$

In this graph

$$\lim_{x \to 0} g(x) = 0 = g(0)$$

but

$$\lim_{x \to 1} g(x) = 1 \neq g(1)$$

and

$$\lim_{x \to -1} g(x) = -1, \text{ but } g(-1) \text{ does not exist.}$$

(Cf. our velocity example to which we referred above: it is just because $g(t_1)$ is not defined that we use $\lim_{x \to t_1} g(x)$ as our definition of v_1.)

Exercise 3

Exercise 3
(4 minutes)

Draw the graphs of the following functions and determine their limits near 1.

(i) g_1, where $g_1 : x \longmapsto x + 1$ $\qquad (x \in R)$

(ii) g_2, where $g_2 : \begin{cases} x \longmapsto x + 1 \text{ if } x \neq 1 \\ x \longmapsto 0 \qquad \text{if } x = 1 \end{cases}$ $\quad (x \in R)$

(iii) g_3, where $g_3 : x \longmapsto \dfrac{(x^2 - 1)}{x - 1}$ $\qquad (x \in R \text{ and } x \neq 1)$ ∎

Exercise 4

Exercise 4
(5 minutes)

Is the following statement true or false? If true, give a demonstration* or proof: if false, give a counter-example.

"If $\lim_{x \to a} f(x) = L$, where a and L are real numbers and f is a real function, and $x_1, x_2, x_3, \ldots$ is a sequence with limit a, none of whose elements is equal to a, then the limit of the sequence $f(x_1), f(x_2), \ldots$ is L." ∎

* By "demonstration" we mean an argument that is not a (rigorous) proof, for example an argument based on a diagram or on an "intuitive definition".

Exercise 5

If a and L are real numbers, and g is a real function then $L = \lim\limits_{x \to a} g(x)$

implies which one of the following?

(i) Given any positive number ε, it is possible to find a positive number δ such that, for all x in $[a - \delta, a + \delta]$ we have $g(x) \in [L - \varepsilon, L + \varepsilon]$.

(ii) For each positive number ε, there exists a positive number δ such that the image under g of the set $\{x : 0 < |x - a| \leqslant \delta\}$ is a subset of $[L - \varepsilon, L + \varepsilon]$.

(iii) $L = g(a)$. ■

Solution 3

(i)

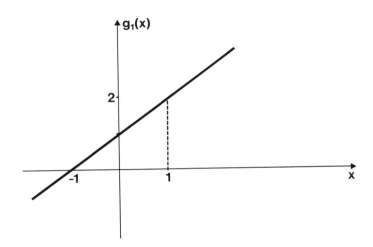

We see that $\lim\limits_{x \to 1} g_1(x) = 2$. In this case $g_1(1)$ exists and also equals 2.

(ii)

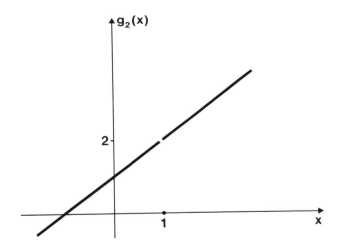

Even though $g_2(1) = 0$ the limit is the same as for (i). In this case $g_2(1)$ exists (its value is 0) but is not the same as $\lim\limits_{x \to 1} g_2(x)$, whose value is 2.

(iii)

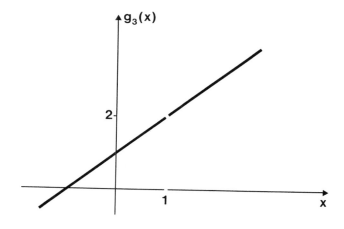

In this case

$$g_3(x) = \frac{x^2 - 1}{x - 1} = \frac{(x - 1)(x + 1)}{x - 1}$$

$$= x + 1$$

(The division by $x - 1$ is legitimate; $x - 1$ is never zero since 1 does not belong to the domain of g_3.) Although $g_3(1)$ is not defined, $\lim_{x \to 1} g_3(x)$ exists and is equal to 2. ∎

Solution 4

Solution 4

The statement is true.

We have two bits of information:

(i) $\lim_{k \, \text{large}} x_k = a,$

(ii) $\lim_{x \to a} f(x) = L.$

Item (i) tells us that

if k is large, then x_k is close to a;

item (ii) tells us that

if x_k is close to a, then $f(x_k)$ is close to L.

Combining them tells us that

if k is large, then $f(x_k)$ is close to L,

or in other words that

$$\lim_{k \, \text{large}} f(x_k) = L.$$ ∎

Solution 5

Alternative (ii) is correct.

Alternative (iii) is wrong because $g(a)$ need not equal $\lim\limits_{x \to a} g(x)$. See (ii) of Exercise 3 for an example where they are different.

Alternative (i) is wrong because it refers to "all x in $[a - \delta, a + \delta]$" when, in fact, the point $x = a$ should be excluded from the set of values of x considered.

Once again (ii) of Exercise 3 gives a counter-example; here we have

$$g(x) = \begin{cases} x + 1 & \text{if } x \neq 1 \\ 0 & \text{if } x = 1 \end{cases} \quad (x \in R)$$

and so, if $x \in [1 - \delta, 1 + \delta]$, then $g(x) \in [2 - \delta, 2 + \delta]$ if $x \neq 1$, but $g(1) = 0$. It follows that, given any small positive ε, it is impossible to find a positive number δ such that, for all x in $[1 - \delta, 1 + \delta], g(x) \in [L - \varepsilon, L + \varepsilon]$ as required by (i).

Alternative (ii) is correct: it differs from (i) only by excluding the point $x = a$ from the set of x-values considered. In fact this statement is the basis of the following more comprehensive definition of $\lim\limits_{x \to a} g(x)$:

A limit of a function g near a point a in its domain is a number L such that for each positive number ε, however small, there is a positive number δ such that the set $\{x : 0 < |x - a| \leqslant \delta \text{ and } x \in \text{the domain of } g\}$ is non-empty, and its image under g is a subset of $[L - \varepsilon, L + \varepsilon]$. ■

7.2.4 Summary

In section 7.2.1 we extended the concept of a finite sequence to that of an infinite sequence.

In section 7.2.2 we defined the limit of an infinite sequence, both intuitively (p. 12) and rigorously (p. 19). We discussed several examples, and found that it is helpful to draw the graph of a sequence when studying its behaviour.

In section 7.2.3 we remarked that a function with domain R^+ is a similar concept to that of an infinite sequence (which is defined by a function with domain Z^+). We defined two types of limit of such a function: the limit for large values of x in its domain (p. 24) and the limit near the point $x = a$, $a \in R^+$ (p. 25).

In Solution 5 (above) we explained that

$$\text{"}L = \lim_{x \to a} g(x)\text{"}$$

is equivalent to the statement:

"Given any positive number ε, there is a positive number δ such that the set

$$\{x : 0 < |x - a| \leqslant \delta \text{ and } x \in \text{the domain of } g\}$$

is non-empty, and its image under g is a subset of

$$[L - \varepsilon, L + \varepsilon].\text{"}$$

7.3 THE EVALUATION OF LIMITS

7.3.0 Introduction

The object of this section is to develop a technique for simplifying the calculation of limits, so that it becomes unnecessary to go right back to the definition of a limit every time we want to evaluate one. The basic idea is that sequences with a complicated rule of formation can be built out of simpler ones by means of operations such as addition and multiplication. If we know how these algebraic operations are reflected in the behaviour of the limits of the sequences, we can evaluate the limits of more complicated sequences in terms of those of simpler ones. In other words we wish to define such things as the sum and the product of two sequences, and (for example) relate the limit of the sum of two sequences to the limits of the individual sequences.

7.3.1 Addition and Multiplication of Sequences

These ideas can be put more precisely using the idea of a morphism, developed in *Unit 3, Operations and Morphisms*. Here we shall be interested in morphisms connected with the function that maps convergent sequences to their limits. We have already foreshadowed the idea of this function when we wrote $\lim u$ for the limit of the sequence u. In fact, if lim is regarded as a function with domain the set of convergent sequences, then we should write $\lim (u)$, but we have chosen to omit the parentheses.

The first algebraic operation we consider is addition. To arrive at a sensible definition for addition of sequences, we use the fact that an infinite sequence is specified by a function with domain Z^+: that is to say, u is specified by the function f where

$$f : k \longmapsto u_k \qquad (k \in Z^+)$$

and v is specified by the function g where

$$g : k \longmapsto v_k \qquad (k \in Z^+)$$

The point of this observation is that we have already given, in *Unit 1, Functions*, the definition for the addition of two functions. Applied to the two functions f and g with domains Z^+, the definition is

$$f + g : k \longmapsto f(k) + g(k) \quad (k \in Z^+)$$

We denote the sequence specified by $f + g$ by $u + v$; so $u + v$ is the sequence

$$u_1 + v_1, u_2 + v_2, u_3 + v_3 \dots$$

That is, to add sequences, we add corresponding elements. For example, if u is $1, 2, 3, 4, \dots$ and v is $1, \frac{1}{2}, \frac{1}{3}, \frac{1}{4}, \dots$, then $u + v$ is $2, 2\frac{1}{2}, 3\frac{1}{3}, 4\frac{1}{4}, \dots$.

Note that the "+" in $u + v$ is really a *new* symbol, denoting the operation "addition of sequences". We use the same symbol as that for the operation "addition of real numbers" because the two operations have similar properties; for example, both operations are commutative and associative.

Exercise 1
(2 minutes)

Exercise 1

If u is $3\frac{1}{2}, 3\frac{1}{3}, 3\frac{1}{4}, 3\frac{1}{5}, \ldots$ and v is $2, 2, 2, 2, \ldots$ what is $u + v$? Also, what are the limits of u, v, and $u + v$, and how are they related? ■

Exercise 2
(4 minutes)

Exercise 2

If u and v are convergent sequences, give a demonstration (i.e. an argument based on the intuitive definition of a limit) that $u + v$ is also convergent and that its limit is $\lim u + \lim v$. ■

Main Text

The result of the last exercise shows two things. First, it shows that the sum of two convergent sequences is another convergent sequence, or in the language of *Unit 3, Operations and Morphisms*, that the set of convergent sequences is closed under addition. Secondly, it shows that there is a morphism in which the operation of adding sequences is carried over by the function lim into the operation of adding numbers (the limits of these sequences). The same fact can be stated schematically as follows:

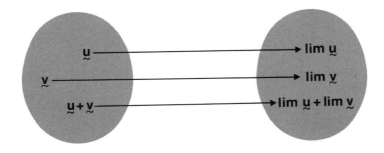

or by the following commutative diagram:

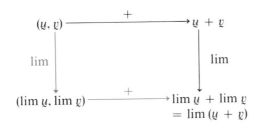

Rule 1
* * *

If we go from the top left-hand to the bottom right-hand corner via the top right-hand corner, we get $\lim(u + v)$, and if we go via the bottom left-hand corner, we get $\lim u + \lim v$, which is the same quantity.

The operation of multiplication can be dealt with in the same way. To define the multiplication of sequences, we again refer back to *Unit 1*, where the product of two functions f and g with domain Z^+ is defined by:

$$f \times g : k \longmapsto f(k) \times g(k) \quad (k \in Z^+)$$

Denoting by $\underset{\sim}{u} \times \underset{\sim}{v}$ the sequence specified by $f \times g$, we see that $\underset{\sim}{u} \times \underset{\sim}{v}$ is the sequence

Notation 3
* * *

$$u_1 \times v_1, u_2 \times v_2, u_3 \times v_3, \ldots$$

i.e. to "multiply" sequences, we multiply corresponding elements. For example, if $\underset{\sim}{u}$ is $1, 2, 3, 4, \ldots$ and $\underset{\sim}{v}$ is $10, 100, 1000, 10\,000, \ldots$, then $\underset{\sim}{u} \times \underset{\sim}{v}$ is $10, 200, 3000, 40\,000, \ldots$. (There are alternative ways to define the "multiplication" of sequences, but in the context of limits, Notation 3 is the useful one because it fits the morphism we wish to develop.)

Note that the "$\times$" in $\underset{\sim}{u} \times \underset{\sim}{v}$ is really a *new* symbol, denoting the operation "multiplication of sequences". We use the same symbol as that for the operation "multiplication of real numbers" because the two operations have similar properties.

Exercise 3

Exercise 3
(3 minutes)

If $\underset{\sim}{u}$ is $0.2, 0.22, 0.222, 0.2222, \ldots$ and $\underset{\sim}{v}$ is $3.3, 3.03, 3.003, 3.0003, \ldots$ what is $\underset{\sim}{u} \times \underset{\sim}{v}$? Also, what are the limits of $\underset{\sim}{u}$, $\underset{\sim}{v}$, and $\underset{\sim}{u} \times \underset{\sim}{v}$, and how are they related? ∎

Exercise 4

Exercise 4
(5 minutes)

If $\underset{\sim}{u}$ and $\underset{\sim}{v}$ are convergent sequences, give a demonstration that $\underset{\sim}{u} \times \underset{\sim}{v}$ is also convergent and that its limit is $(\lim \underset{\sim}{u}) \times (\lim \underset{\sim}{v})$. ∎

Like the result of Exercise 2, this last one shows us two things: that the set of convergent sequences is closed under multiplication, and that there is a morphism in which the operation of multiplying two sequences is carried over into the operation of multiplying their limits.

Discussion

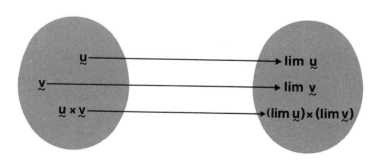

Solution 1

The sequence $u + v$ is $5\frac{1}{2}, 5\frac{1}{3}, 5\frac{1}{4}, 5\frac{1}{5}, \ldots$. The limit of u is 3 and the limit of v is 2. Also, from the sequence $u + v$ as written out above, we see that the limit of $u + v$ is 5. These limits are connected by the relationship

$$\lim u + \lim v = \lim (u + v) \qquad \blacksquare$$

Solution 2

"u is convergent" means that we can find $N \in Z^+$ such that u_k is as close to $\lim u$ as we please for all $k > N$.

"v is convergent" means that we can find $M \in Z^+$ such that v_k is as close to $\lim v$ as we please for all $k > M$.

Intuitively, this means that we can find $P \in Z^+$ such that $u_k + v_k$ is as close to $\lim u + \lim v$ as we please for all $k > P$, where P depends on N and M; that is, $u + v$ is convergent to $\lim u + \lim v$.

This also suggests a rigorous line of proof: see Appendix I. $\qquad \blacksquare$

Solution 3

Multiplying the two sequences together we get the sequence

$$0.66, 0.6666, 0.666666, \ldots$$

Now $\lim u = 0.2222 \ldots = \frac{2}{9}$ and $\lim v = 3$.

Also, from the sequence that we have just obtained, we have

$$\lim (u \times v) = 0.6666 \ldots = \frac{2}{3}$$

so that

$$\lim u \times \lim v = \lim (u \times v)$$

since $\frac{2}{9} \times 3 = \frac{2}{3}$. $\qquad \blacksquare$

Solution 4

We proceed in exactly the same way as in Exercise 2. We can find integers $N, M \in Z^+$ such that u_k is as close to $\lim u$ as we please for all $k > N$, and v_k is as close to $\lim v$ as we please for all $k > M$. Intuitively, this means that we can find $P \in Z^+$ such that $u_k \times v_k$ is as close to $(\lim u) \times (\lim v)$ as we please for all $k > P$, where P depends on N and M; that is, $u \times v$ is convergent and

$$\lim (u \times v) = (\lim u) \times (\lim v)$$

This is the multiplication rule for limits. It can be proved, using the rigorous definition of a limit, but we shall not give the details here. $\qquad \blacksquare$

Rule 2
* * *

Exercise 5

Draw the commutative diagram for the operation of multiplication and the function "lim".

Exercise 5
(3 minutes)

■

Exercise 6

Use the addition and multiplication rules for limits to evaluate:

Exercise 6
(5 minutes)

(i) $\lim\limits_{k\ \text{large}} \left(4 + \dfrac{1}{k}\right)$

(ii) $\lim\limits_{k\ \text{large}} (2^{-k} + \pi_k)$

where π_k denotes π rounded off to k places of decimals, i.e.

$$\pi_1 = 3.1$$

$$\pi_2 = 3.14$$

$$\pi_3 = 3.142, \text{ etc.}$$

(iii) $\lim\limits_{k\ \text{large}} (\underbrace{0.333\ldots3}_{k\ \text{digits}} \times \pi_k)$

(iv) $\lim\limits_{k\ \text{large}} v_k^2$

where $v_1, v_2, \ldots$ is any convergent sequence. Express your answer in terms of lim v.

(HINT: write v_k^2 as $v_k \times v_k$).

(v) $\lim\limits_{k\ \text{large}} \left(2 + \dfrac{1}{k}\right)\left(3 + \dfrac{2}{k}\right)$

■

7.3.2 Composition of Functions and Continuity

7.3.2

Main Text
* * *

The third way of combining functions discussed in *Unit 1*, as well as addition and multiplication, was composition. This also has its place in the theory of limits. It enables us to define functions that act on sequences. For example, we could define the square of the sequence $1, 2, 3, \ldots$ to be the result of multiplying this sequence by itself, which we have already defined to be $1 \times 1, 2 \times 2, 3 \times 3, \ldots$ or $1^2, 2^2, 3^2 \ldots$. We can think of this new sequence as produced by the "square it" function

$$x \longmapsto x^2 \quad (x \in R)$$

acting on the sequence $1, 2, \ldots$. There is nothing special about either the function or the sequence used in this example; in general, we may take any sequence of numbers $u_1, u_2, u_3 \ldots$ and any function g with domain and codomain R, and then the function g is said to act on the sequence u to give the new sequence

$$g(u_1), g(u_2), g(u_3), \ldots$$

which we shall abbreviate to $g(u)$.

Notation 1
* * *

The relation of this to the composition of functions can be seen by introducing the function specifying the sequence u, which is

$$f: k \longmapsto u_k \quad (k \in Z^+)$$

Using this function we can write $g(u)$ in the alternative form

$$g(f(1)), g(f(2)), g(f(3)), \ldots$$

or in terms of the composite function $g \circ f$ defined by $g \circ f: x \longmapsto g(f(x))$ $(x \in Z^+)$:

$$g \circ f(1), g \circ f(2), \ldots$$

(continued on page 36)

Solution 7.3.1.5

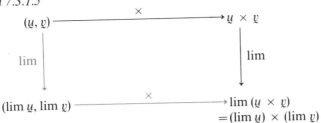

Solution 7.3.1.6

In (i) and (ii) below we use the addition rule

$$\lim u + \lim v = \lim (u + v)$$

In (iii) and (iv) we use the multiplication rule

$$(\lim u) \times (\lim v) = \lim (u \times v)$$

In (v) we combine both these rules.

(i) $\displaystyle \lim_{k \text{ large}} \left(4 + \frac{1}{k}\right) = \lim (4 + 1, 4\frac{1}{2}, 4\frac{1}{3}, \dots)$

$$= \lim (4, 4, 4, \dots) + \lim (1, \tfrac{1}{2}, \tfrac{1}{3}, \dots)$$

$$= 4 + 0 = 4$$

(ii) $\displaystyle \lim_{k \text{ large}} (2^{-k} + \pi_k) = \lim_{k \text{ large}} (2^{-k}) + \lim_{k \text{ large}} (\pi_k)$

$$= 0 + \pi = \pi$$

(iii) $\displaystyle \lim_{k \text{ large}} (\underbrace{0.33 \dots 3}_{k \text{ digits}} \times \pi_k) = \lim_{k \text{ large}} (\underbrace{0.33 \dots 3}_{k \text{ digits}}) \times \lim_{k \text{ large}} (\pi_k)$

$$= \frac{1}{3} \times \pi = \frac{\pi}{3}$$

(iv) $\displaystyle \lim_{k \text{ large}} (v_k^2) = \lim_{k \text{ large}} (v_k \times v_k)$

$$= (\lim_{k \text{ large}} v_k) \times (\lim_{k \text{ large}} v_k) = (\lim v)^2$$

(v) $\displaystyle \lim_{k \text{ large}} \left(2 + \frac{1}{k}\right) \times \left(3 + \frac{2}{k}\right) = \lim_{k \text{ large}} \left(2 + \frac{1}{k}\right) \times \lim_{k \text{ large}} \left(3 + \frac{2}{k}\right)$

$$= 2 \times 3 = 6$$

(*continued from page 35*)

This shows that if the function specifying the sequence u is f, then the one specifying the sequence $g(u)$ is $g \circ f$.

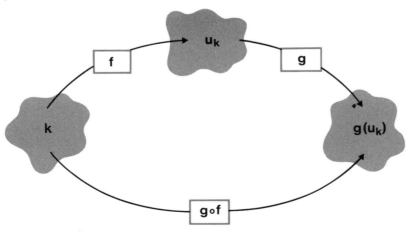

Sequences of the type $g(u)$ are important in the theory of iterative computation methods. For example, we have already considered (in 7.1.2 of this text) Newton's method for computing successive approximations to the square root of some given positive number a; it is defined by the recurrence formula

$$u_k = \frac{1}{2}\left(u_{k-1} + \frac{a}{u_{k-1}}\right) \quad (k = 2, 3, \dots)$$

The right-hand side of this equation can be regarded as the image of the number u_{k-1} under the function g, where

$$g(x) = \frac{1}{2}\left(x + \frac{a}{x}\right) \qquad (x \in R \text{ and } x \neq 0)$$

Equation (1)

and so Newton's formula can be written

$$u_k = g(u_{k-1}) \qquad (k = 2, 3, 4, \dots)$$

To find the limit of the sequence generated by a recurrence formula of this form, we can take the limit of both sides of it, and for this we would like to relate the limiting properties of the sequence u to those of the sequence $g(u)$.

The general question here is whether, for any real function g, the sequence $g(u)$ converges, and if so, what is its limit. Before jumping to any conclusions, look at the following example, which shows that even when u converges, $g(u)$ may not.

Example 1

We take u to be

Example 1

$$-1, \tfrac{1}{2}, -\tfrac{1}{3}, \tfrac{1}{4}, \dots$$

We take g to be the function whose graph is shown

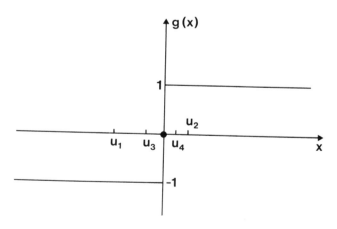

It is sometimes called the sign (not sine) function, since $g(x)$ has the sign, but not the magnitude, of x. Its formal definition is

$$g : x \longmapsto \begin{cases} +1 & \text{if } x > 0 \\ 0 & \text{if } x = 0 \\ -1 & \text{if } x < 0 \end{cases} \quad (x \in R)$$

The sequences u and $g(u)$ are therefore

$$\left. \begin{aligned} u &: -1, \tfrac{1}{2}, -\tfrac{1}{3}, \tfrac{1}{4}, \dots \\ g(u) &: -1, 1, -1, 1, \dots \end{aligned} \right\}$$

and although u converges (to the limit 0), $g(u)$ does not. ■

Example 2

Example 2

On the other hand, there are many cases where $g(\underline{u})$ does converge; for example, if g were $x \longmapsto x^2$ $(x \in R)$, then with $\underline{u}$ as before:

$$\underline{u} : -1, \tfrac{1}{2}, -\tfrac{1}{3}, \tfrac{1}{4}, -\tfrac{1}{5}, \ldots$$

and

$$g(\underline{u}) : 1, \tfrac{1}{4}, \tfrac{1}{9}, \tfrac{1}{16}, \tfrac{1}{25}, \ldots$$

which converges to the limit 0. ■

Main Text
* * *

The essential difference between these two examples is that in the first the graph of g has a gap at $x = 0$, whereas in the second it has none (see below):

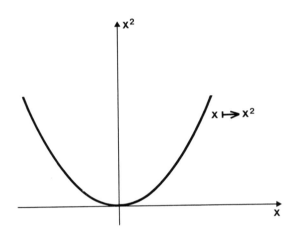

To formulate a general result about sequences of the form $g(\underline{u})$, we therefore first look more closely at the implications of gaps in a graph. The gap in the graph in Example 1 has the effect that if x is close to 0 then a very small change in x can produce a change of magnitude of 1 or 2 in $g(x)$. For example, for the two consecutive integers k and $k + 1$, where $k = 10^6$, $u_k = \dfrac{1}{10^6}$ and $u_{k+1} = -\dfrac{1}{10^6 + 1}$. We may regard both these numbers as very close to 0, but $g(u_k) = 1$ and $g(u_{k+1}) = -1$.

On the other hand, if the graph of g does not have a gap, as in Example 2, then a small change in x necessarily produces only a small change in $g(x)$. In this case we expect that, for large k, $g(u_k)$ will be close to $g(\lim \underline{u})$, and so the sequence $g(\underline{u})$ will converge and have the limit $g(\lim \underline{u})$. A function whose graph has a gap at $x = a$ is said to be discontinuous at a; if there is no gap at a it is said to be continuous at a. Thus the sign function whose graph is shown in Example 1 is discontinuous at 0, but continuous at all other points (elements) in its domain; the function $x \longmapsto x^2$ $(x \in R)$ is continuous everywhere in its domain.

Intuitive Definition 1
* * *
Intuitive Definition 2
* * *

For a precise definition of continuity, the concept of limit of a function at a point serves admirably. For any real function f, we have defined the limit of f near a to be a number L such that if x is very close, but not equal, to a, then $f(x)$ is very close to L. If this limit exists, therefore, and a is in the domain of f, then the only possible gap in the graph when x is close to a is a displaced point at $x = a$ itself.

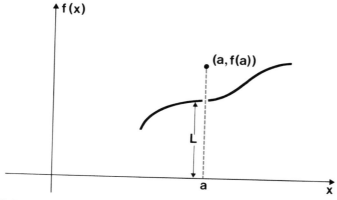

Thus, if the limit near *a* not only exists but is equal to *f*(*a*), then the function has no gaps at *a* and may therefore be said to be continuous at *a*. Accordingly we make the

> ### Definition of Continuity
>
> If *f* is a real function and *a* is an element of its domain, then "*f* is continuous at *a*" is equivalent to the statement "$\lim_{x \to a} f(x)$ exists and is equal to *f*(*a*)".

Definition 3
* * *

Notice that we now require *a* to belong to the domain, whereas in defining $\lim_{x \to a} f(x)$ we did not; by this definition, if *f*(*a*) is undefined (i.e. if *a* does not belong to the domain), then *f* is not continuous at *a*. Thus the definition fits our intuitive ideas of continuity in this case too, since the graph must have a gap at *a* if *f*(*a*) is undefined.

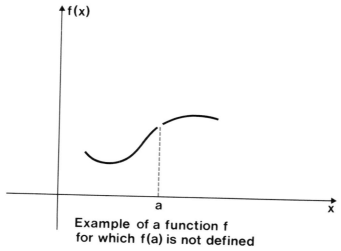

Example of a function f
for which f(a) is not defined

The practical way of discovering whether a function is continuous or not is to sketch its graph. For example, here are graphs of a few functions:

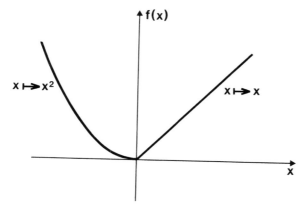

$$f:x \longmapsto \begin{Bmatrix} x & \text{if } x \geqslant 0 \\ x^2 & \text{if } x < 0 \end{Bmatrix} \quad (x \in R)$$

is continuous throughout its domain.

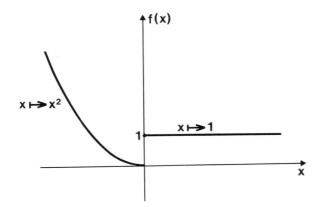

$$f:x \longmapsto \begin{Bmatrix} 1 & \text{if } x \geqslant 0 \\ x^2 & \text{if } x < 0 \end{Bmatrix} \quad (x \in R)$$

is discontinuous at 0 (because of the jump), but continuous elsewhere.

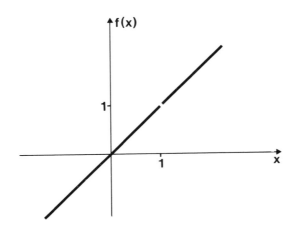

$$f:x \longmapsto x \quad (x \in R \text{ and } x \neq 1)$$

is discontinuous at 1 (because of the gap in the domain), but continuous elsewhere.

Exercise 1

Exercise 1
(4 minutes)

Which of the following functions are continuous at 0?

(i) h_1, where $h_1 : \begin{Bmatrix} x \longmapsto x & \text{if } x \geqslant 0 \\ x \longmapsto 0 & \text{if } x < 0 \end{Bmatrix} \quad (x \in R)$

(ii) h_2, where $h_2 : \begin{Bmatrix} x \longmapsto \dfrac{|x|}{x} & \text{if } x \neq 0 \\ x \longmapsto 1 & \text{if } x = 0 \end{Bmatrix} \quad (x \in R)$

(iii) h_3, where $h_3 : x \longmapsto \dfrac{1}{x^2}$ $(x \in R \text{ and } x \neq 0)$

(iv) h_4, where $h_4 : x \longmapsto 1$ $(x \in R \text{ and } x \neq 0)$ ■

We can now return to the question that led us to consider the concept of continuity: "If u is a convergent sequence and g is a real function, does the sequence $g(u)$ converge?"

The answer is that, if g is continuous at $\lim u$, then the sequence does converge, and its limit is $g(\lim u)$. This is demonstrated in the diagram below:

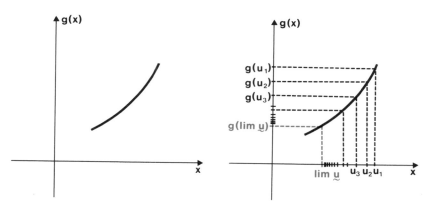

As k increases, the numbers u_k approach the value $\lim u$, and at the same time the numbers $g(u_k)$ approach the value $g(\lim u)$, so that the limit of the sequence $g(u_1), g(u_2), g(u_3)$, is $g(\lim u)$. A concise statement of this result is this:

> If g is continuous at $\lim u$, then $g(u)$ converges and
> $$\lim g(u) = g(\lim u)$$

We call it the continuous function rule for limits.

This result generalizes that of Example 2 where we showed that if $u_1, u_2, u_3, \ldots$ is a convergent sequence with limit a, none of whose elements are equal to a, and if $\lim_{x \to a} g(x)$ exists, then the sequence $g(u)$ converges to the limit $\lim_{x \to a} g(x)$. Rule 1 states that if in addition the function g is continuous at a, so that $g(a) = \lim_{x \to a} g(x)$, then the uncomfortable restriction that no element of u may equal a can be dropped.

Here is an example of how Rule 1 can be used in finding limits of sequences:

Example 3

Example 3

Find $\lim_{k \text{ large}} \left(\dfrac{1}{4 + 2^{-k}} \right)$

One can find this limit either intuitively or by means of the continuous function rule. Intuitively we can argue this way: when k is very large, 2^{-k} is very small; so $4 + 2^{-k}$ is very close to 4; so $\dfrac{1}{(4 + 2^{-k})}$ is very close to $\frac{1}{4}$, so the limit is $\frac{1}{4}$.

To use the continuous function rule, we want to find a convergent sequence $u_1, u_2, \ldots$ and a real function g, continuous at $\lim u$, such that

$$\frac{1}{4 + 2^{-k}} = g(u_k) \quad (k = 1, 2, \ldots)$$

A convenient choice is

$$u_k = 2^{-k} \qquad (k = 1, 2, \ldots)$$

$$g(x) = \frac{1}{4 + x} \qquad (x \in R \text{ and } x \neq -4)$$

(*continued on page 42*)

Solution 1

h_1 is the only function listed that is continuous at 0. Its graph is:

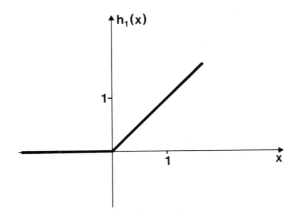

Since $|x| = x$ for $x > 0$ but $|x| = -x$ for $x < 0$, the graph of h_2 is:

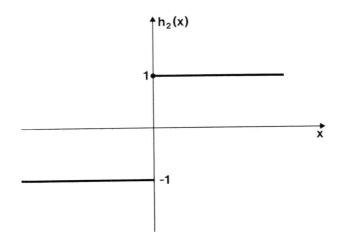

which has a gap at $x = 0$, and so h_2 is not continuous at 0.

h_3 and h_4 are not continuous at 0 since the functions are not defined there.

∎

(continued from page 41)

because 2^{-k} is the only k-dependent part of $\dfrac{1}{4 + 2^{-k}}$, and we know that $\lim\limits_{k\,\text{large}} (2^{-k})$ is 0. The function g is continuous at $x = 0$ (its only discontinuity is at $x = -4$, the zero of the denominator, where there is a gap in the domain). Accordingly we have

$$\left.\begin{aligned}\lim g(u) &= g(\lim u)\\ &= g(0)\end{aligned}\right\} \text{since } \lim u = 0 \text{ and } g \text{ is continuous at 0.}$$

$$= \frac{1}{4 + 0} \quad \text{by definition of } g.$$

$$= \frac{1}{4} \qquad\qquad\qquad ∎$$

Exercise 2

Evaluate the following limits of sequences by using Rule 1:

(i) $\lim\limits_{k\,\text{large}} \sin\left(\dfrac{1}{k}\right) \quad (k \in Z^+)$

(ii) $\lim\limits_{k\,\text{large}} \dfrac{1}{3 + \frac{1}{k}} \qquad (k \in Z^+)$

■

7.3.3 Application of the Rules

Sometimes a little ingenuity is necessary before the rules of addition, multiplication, and composition can be applied. For example, to evaluate the limit of the sequence

$$w = \frac{5}{-1}, \frac{8}{3}, \frac{11}{7}, \ldots, \frac{3k+2}{4k-5}, \ldots$$

it is no good writing the general element w_k as the product of $3k + 2$ and $\dfrac{1}{4k-5}$ because the sequence $u_k = 3k + 2$ does not converge. We can, however, divide the numerator and denominator of each term by k, so that the sequence is now rewritten

$$\frac{5}{-1}, \frac{\frac{8}{2}}{\frac{3}{2}}, \frac{\frac{11}{3}}{\frac{7}{3}}, \ldots, \frac{3 + \frac{2}{k}}{4 - \frac{5}{k}}, \ldots$$

The general element of the sequence can now be written as the product of $3 + \dfrac{2}{k}$ and $\dfrac{1}{4 - 5/k}$, whose limits are 3 and $\frac{1}{4}$ respectively, so that $\lim w = \frac{3}{4}$.

The same method can be applied to any convergent sequence of fractions where the denominator of the general element of the sequence is the sum of several terms: before taking the limit we divide the numerator and denominator of each element of the sequence by the term in the denominator that is largest for very large k. This term is called the dominant term in the denominator.

Exercise 1

Evaluate the following limits:

(i) $\lim\limits_{n\,\text{large}} \left\{ \dfrac{n^{-1} - 5n^{-3}}{4n^{-1} + 6n^{-2}} \right\}$ (the dominant term is $4n^{-1}$)

(ii) $\lim\limits_{n\,\text{large}} \left(\dfrac{n^2 + 5n - 2}{3n^2 - n + 1} \right)$

(iii) $\lim\limits_{k\,\text{large}} \left(\dfrac{6 + 2^{k-1}}{2^k + 1} \right)$

■

Solution 7.3.2.2 **Solution 7.3.2.2**

(i) Define $u_k = \dfrac{1}{k}$ $(k = 1, 2, \ldots)$

Then $\lim\limits_{k \text{ large}} \sin \dfrac{1}{k} = \lim (\sin u)$. Since $\lim u = 0$ and the sine function is continuous at 0 (by its graph), we have

$$\lim (\sin u) = \sin (\lim u) = \sin 0 = 0$$

(ii) Define u_k as in (i) and let $g : x \longmapsto \dfrac{1}{3 + x}$ $(x \in R$ and $x \neq -3)$.

Then $\lim\limits_{k \text{ large}} \left(\dfrac{1}{3 + \frac{1}{k}} \right) = \lim\limits_{k \text{ large}} (g(u_k)) = \lim g(u)$. By its graph, the function

$x \longmapsto \dfrac{1}{3 + x}$ is continuous at 0 and so

$$\lim g(u) = g(\lim u) = g(0) = \frac{1}{3 + 0} = \frac{1}{3}$$

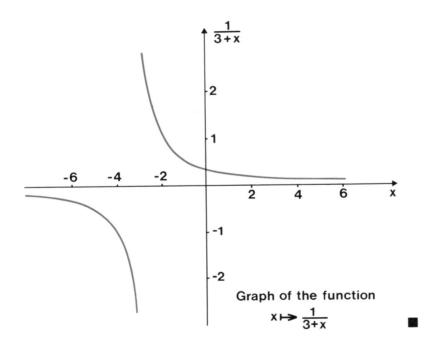

Graph of the function

$x \mapsto \dfrac{1}{3+x}$ ■

Solution 1 **Solution 1**

(i) The limit is $\frac{1}{4}$.

If we divide numerator and denominator by $4n^{-1}$ (i.e. multiply by $\frac{1}{4}n$), then we get the fraction

$$\frac{\dfrac{1}{4} - \dfrac{5}{4n^2}}{1 + \dfrac{6}{4n}}$$

For large n, the numerator is very close to $\frac{1}{4}$ and the denominator is very close to 1, so that the quotient is very close to $\frac{1}{4}$. By making n large enough we can make the error in this approximation as small as we please, and so the exact value of the limit is $\frac{1}{4}$.

(ii) Neither the numerator nor the denominator of the fraction is the general term of a convergent sequence. However, when we divide both by $3n^2$ we get

$$\frac{\dfrac{1}{3} + \dfrac{5}{3n} - \dfrac{2}{3n^2}}{1 - \dfrac{1}{3n} + \dfrac{1}{3n^2}}$$

For large n the numerator is very close to $\frac{1}{3}$ and the denominator very close to 1, so the fraction as a whole is very close to $\frac{1}{3}$. By making n large enough we can make the error in this approximation as small as we please; so the exact value of the limit is $\frac{1}{3}$.

(iii) $\lim\limits_{k \text{ large}} \left\{ k \longmapsto \left(\dfrac{6 + 2^{k-1}}{2^k + 1} \right) \right\}$ (dominant term is 2^k)

$$= \lim\limits_{k \text{ large}} \left\{ k \longmapsto \left(\frac{\frac{6}{2^k} + \frac{1}{2}}{1 + \frac{1}{2^k}} \right) \right\}$$

$$= \frac{\frac{1}{2}}{1} = \frac{1}{2} \qquad \blacksquare$$

7.3.4   Limits of Sequences Defined by Recurrence Formulas

In section 7.1.2 we considered the applications of sequences to computing, and we saw that sequences specified by recurrence formulas such as

$$u_k = F(u_{k-1})$$

(with some given u_1) are particularly convenient in these applications. An example is the recurrence formula of Newton's square-root process

$$u_k = \frac{1}{2}\left(u_{k-1} + \frac{a}{u_{k-1}} \right)$$

which we have discussed earlier in this text. For this process, the function F is given by

$$F(x) = \frac{1}{2}\left(x + \frac{a}{x} \right) \qquad (x \in R \text{ and } x \neq 0)$$

Using the result on limits of sequences of the form $g(u)$ from section 7.3.2, we can evaluate the limits of sequences specified in this way.

The above general recurrence formula really means that $u_k = F(u_{k-1})$ is true for $k = 2, 3, \ldots$ and therefore that the sequences

$$\left. \begin{aligned} &u_2, u_3, u_4, \ldots \\ &F(u_1), F(u_2), \ldots \end{aligned} \right\}$$

and

are identical. Let us make the assumption that u converges; then the sequence $u_2, u_3, \ldots$ (i.e. u with u_1 left out) also converges, and its limit is $\lim u$ (this can be checked using the definition of a limit). It follows that the sequence $F(u_1), F(u_2), \ldots$ also has the limit $\lim u$. In the notation we used in section 7.3.2, this statement is

$$\lim F(u) = \lim u$$

If we make the further assumption that F is continuous at $\lim u$, then the result $\lim F(u) = F(\lim u)$, found on page 41, gives

$$\lim u = F(\lim u)$$

Equation (1)

That is, on the assumptions that u converges and that F is continuous at $\lim u$, we can find $\lim u$ by solving Equation (1).

As an example, we have just seen that in Newton's square-root process the function F is given by $F(x) = \frac{1}{2}\left(x + \frac{a}{x}\right)$, and so Equation (1) implies that for this process the limit of the sequence satisfies

$$\lim u = \frac{1}{2}\left(\lim u + \frac{a}{\lim u}\right)$$

provided u converges and $\lim u \neq 0$. (This last condition ensures the continuity of F at $\lim u$, since its only discontinuity is at 0.) On multiplying both sides of the last equation by $\lim u$ and simplifying, we obtain the quadratic equation

$$(\lim u)^2 = a$$

which leads to

$$\lim u = \pm\sqrt{a}$$

Thus the sequence given by Newton's square-root method, if it converges to any limit other than zero, must converge either to $+\sqrt{a}$ or to $-\sqrt{a}$. When we used Newton's method in 7.1.2, we found that the sequence did appear to converge to a non-zero limit, and that its elements were positive (this is because u_1 was chosen positive), and so $\lim u$ for this process is indeed $\sqrt{a}$, the quantity the method is intended to calculate.

The main importance of the formula $\lim u = F(\lim u)$, however, is not in evaluating the limit of a sequence with a known recurrence relation, but in solving equations iteratively. In *Unit 2, Errors and Accuracy*, we showed how to construct a sequence of successive approximations to a solution of the equation

$$x^3 - 5x + 3 = 0$$

by rearranging it into a form such as

$$x = \tfrac{1}{5}(x^3 + 3)$$

and then constructing a sequence from the recurrence formula

$$u_k = \tfrac{1}{5}(u_{k-1}^3 + 3) \quad (k = 2, 3, \ldots)$$

with some initial guess for u_1. In general, the method is to rearrange the equation we are trying to solve into the form

$$x = F(x)$$

where the function F is different for different rearrangements of the same equation, and then to construct a sequence using the recurrence formula

$$u_k = F(u_{k-1}) \quad (k = 2, 3, \ldots)$$

We saw in *Unit 2* that, depending on the rearrangement chosen and the initial guess u_1, this sequence sometimes diverges wildly, but sometimes it can be used to calculate an approximate solution of the original equation $x = F(x)$. The limit concept tells us that, in principle, the recurrence formula can give not only approximations but also an exact solution of the equation (in the sense that if the sequence converges then its limit is an exact solution). This idea greatly simplifies the theory of the iterative method, since once we have the limit concept we no longer need to waste time on approximate solutions and their error estimates but can work directly from the exact solution. (Of course, in practical computations as opposed to theory, we can never escape from approximations, but this does not detract from the importance of the exact solution as a base from which to study the effectiveness of the iterative method.) We shall be returning to the theory of the iterative method later in the course.

7.3.5 Summary

In this section we discussed the evaluation of limits of complicated sequences in terms of limits of simpler ones.

In section 7.3.1 we defined addition and multiplication of two sequences, u and v say, and gave the following rules:

If u and v are convergent to $\lim u$ and $\lim v$ respectively, then

 (i) the sequence $u + v$ is convergent to $\lim u + \lim v$;

(ii) the sequence $u \times v$ is convergent to $\lim u \times \lim v$.

In section 7.3.2 we discussed the composition of sequences. If u is the sequence defined by $f : k \longmapsto u_k$ $(k \in Z^+)$ and g is a real function, then we defined $g(u)$ to be the sequence $g(f(1)), g(f(2)), g(f(3)), \ldots$. We gave an example illustrating that if u is convergent then $g(u)$ does not necessarily converge. This led us to the concept of continuity of a function (p. 39): a function is continuous at $x = a$ if its graph has no "gap" at $x = a$. We stated the rule: If u is convergent to $\lim u$ and g is continuous at $\lim u$, then $g(u)$ is convergent to $g(\lim u)$.

Finally, we illustrated these rules by examples.

7.4 THE EXPONENTIAL FUNCTION

7.4.0 Introduction

As an illustration of the power of the concept of a limit we shall next give an example which shows how this concept can be used to define new numbers and new functions, which cannot be defined using only the finite processes of ordinary arithmetic. The function we shall consider is called the exponential function.

7.4.1 Population Growth

The significance of the exponential function is that it provides the simplest mathematical representation for growth processes and also for decay processes. An example is the growth of the world's population: the "population explosion". We can set up a mathematical model of this by denoting the time (i.e. the number of years that have elapsed since some designated initial instant) by t, the population at time t by $f(t)$ (i.e. f is the function that maps the time to the population at that time), and the birth and death rates per annum per head of population by b and d. We assume for simplicity that b and d are constants. As a first step towards determining how $f(t)$ depends on t, let us look at the population changes during a single year, lasting from, say, time t_0 to $t_0 + 1$. The calculation can be laid out in this way (the sign $\simeq$ means "approximately equals"):

number alive at time t_0 $= f(t_0)$;

number born between t_0 and $t_0 + 1$ $\simeq bf(t_0)$;

number dying between t_0 and $t_0 + 1$ $\simeq df(t_0)$;

number alive at time $t_0 + 1$ $\simeq f(t_0) + bf(t_0) - df(t_0)$

i.e.

$$f(t_0 + 1) \simeq (1 + x)f(t_0)$$

Equation (1)

where we define x, the net rate of population increase per annum per head of population, by

$$x = (b - d)$$

Can you see why we used the sign "$\simeq$" instead of "$=$"? The inaccuracy is that we have calculated the births and deaths as if the population had the constant value $f(t_0)$ throughout the year. For a more accurate calculation we should allow for the fact that $f(t)$ increases throughout the year, so that the population is greater in the second half year than in the first, and consequently (with constant birth and death rates) there are more births and deaths in the second half of the year than in the first. One way to do this is to consider the two halves of the year separately as shown below:

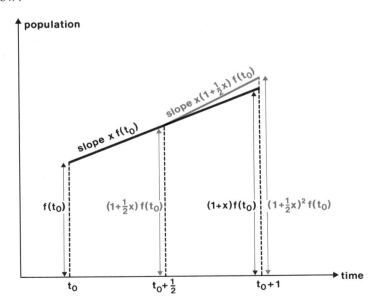

Black: This part is based on the assumption that there is a steady rate of increase of population throughout the year.

Red: This part is based on the assumption that there is a faster rate of increase of population in the second half-year.

For the first half-year the calculation is

number alive at time t_0 $= f(t_0)$

number born in the first half year $\simeq \frac{1}{2}bf(t_0)$;

number dying in first half year $\simeq \frac{1}{2}df(t_0)$;

number alive at time $t_0 + \frac{1}{2}$ $\simeq (1 + \frac{1}{2}b - \frac{1}{2}d)f(t_0)$,

so that

$$f(t_0 + \tfrac{1}{2}) \simeq (1 + \tfrac{1}{2}x)f(t_0)$$

By a similar calculation starting halfway through the year, we find:

$$f(t_0 + 1) \simeq (1 + \tfrac{1}{2}x)f(t_0 + \tfrac{1}{2});$$

substituting for $f(t_0 + \frac{1}{2})$ from our previous equation yields

$$f(t_0 + 1) \simeq (1 + \tfrac{1}{2}x)^2 f(t_0)$$

Equation (2)

This is a more accurate result than Equation (1), though it is still approximate because we have assumed that there are as many births in the first quarter year as the second and as many in the third quarter as the fourth.

To improve the approximation still further we could divide the year into four parts. Then a similar calculation to the one above gives

$$f(t_0 + \tfrac{1}{4}) \simeq (1 + \tfrac{1}{4}x)f(t_0)$$
$$f(t_0 + \tfrac{1}{2}) \simeq (1 + \tfrac{1}{4}x)f(t_0 + \tfrac{1}{4})$$
$$f(t_0 + \tfrac{3}{4}) \simeq (1 + \tfrac{1}{4}x)f(t_0 + \tfrac{1}{2})$$
$$f(t_0 + 1) \simeq (1 + \tfrac{1}{4}x)f(t_0 + \tfrac{3}{4})$$

Combining the four equations gives

$$f(t_0 + 1) \simeq (1 + \tfrac{1}{4}x)^4 f(t_0)$$

Equation (3)

This is more accurate than Equation (2), though still approximate.

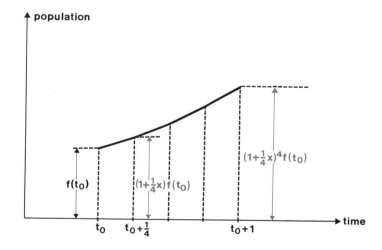

By further subdividing the year in this fashion into more and more parts we can obtain even better approximations to $f(t_0 + 1)$; subdividing the year into k equal parts gives

$$f(t_0 + 1) \simeq \left(1 + \frac{x}{k}\right)^k f(t_0)$$

Equation (4)

By making the number of subdivisions, k, very large, we would expect to get a very good approximation from this formula. The "intuitive" definition of a limit tells us that $f(t_0 + 1)$ is given as accurately as possible by the limit of the sequence of successive approximations.

In symbols, it tells us that

$$f(t_0 + 1) = \lim_{k \text{ large}} \left(1 + \frac{x}{k}\right)^k f(t_0)$$

This formula, which is exact within the restrictions of our model of population growth, solves the problem posed at the beginning of this section, by telling us that over 1 year the population increases by a factor which is the limit of the sequence

$$1 + x, (1 + \tfrac{1}{2}x)^2, (1 + \tfrac{1}{3}x)^3, \ldots$$

The importance of this limit goes far beyond the particular problem used here to introduce it. It has many applications in science, engineering and social science, as well as in mathematics itself. To give you an idea of how the sequence behaves, here are the first 10 elements in the cases $x = 0.1$ and $x = 1$.

k	$\left(1 + \dfrac{0.1}{k}\right)^k$	$\left(1 + \dfrac{1}{k}\right)^k$
1	1.1	2
2	1.1025	2.25
3	1.103370	2.370370
4	1.103813	2.441406
5	1.104081	2.488320
6	1.104260	2.521626
7	1.104389	2.546500
8	1.104486	2.565785
9	1.104561	2.581175
10	1.104622	2.593742

For $x = 0.1$, the sequence converges fairly rapidly and the limit is 1.105 to 3 decimal places. For $x = 1$ the convergence is slower, but by taking the calculation far enough we would obtain any desired accuracy. (A proof that the sequence really does converge is given in Appendix II.) The value of the limit when $x = 1$ is a number whose frequency of occurrence in mathematical work rivals that of π. It is denoted by e, and to 5 decimal places its value is

$$e = 2.71828$$

The value of the limit for other values of x also appears very frequently. The function that maps x to the value of this limit is called the exponential function, and denoted by exp, so that

Definition 1
* * *

$$\exp : x \longmapsto \lim_{k \text{ large}} \left(1 + \frac{x}{k}\right)^k \quad (x \in R)$$

and

$$\exp(x) = \lim_{k \text{ large}} \left(1 + \frac{x}{k}\right)^k \quad (x \in R)$$

We often abbreviate $\exp(x)$ to $\exp x$.

The graph of this function is shown on the next page.

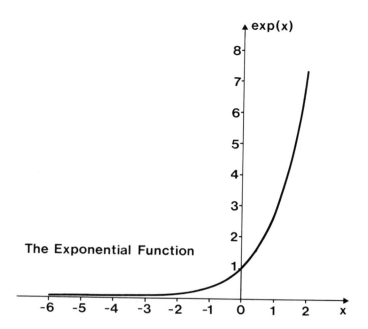

The Exponential Function

We see from the graph that exp x is *positive* for *all* values of x.

Exercise 1

Use the information given on the last few pages to evaluate

$$\exp(0), \exp(1) \text{ and } \exp\left(\tfrac{1}{10}\right)$$

to 3 decimal places.

■

Exercise 1
(5 minutes)

Exercise 2

In Exercise 7.1.2.3 you obtained the recurrence formula

$$u_k = \left(1 + \frac{r}{100}\right)u_{k-1}$$

for the balance at the end of the kth year in an inactive account at a savings bank, where the interest rate is $r\%$ compounded annually. What is the recurrence formula relating u_k to u_{k-1} if interest at the rate of $r\%$ per annum is compounded (i) half-yearly (ii) quarterly (iii) monthly?

Exercise 2
(3 minutes)

7.4.2 The Exponential Theorem

7.4.2

You may have wondered why we used the name "exponential" for the function we discussed in the preceding section. The reason is that it is closely related to the idea of an exponent (an exponent is a number telling us to raise some other number to a power, for example the 2 in 5^2 or the 6 in 10^6). In this section we state a theorem which exhibits this relationship. The theorem itself (particularly in the form stated in Equation (2) below) is important, but the proof is less so, and it therefore appears in Appendix III. We would like you to read and understand it; but if you do not, it will not affect either your assessment or your understanding of the rest of the course.

Discussion

A special case of the theorem is

$$\exp\left(\frac{p}{q}\right) = e^{p/q} \quad (p \in Z, q \in Z^+)*$$

Equation (1)

* For example, we write $-\frac{1}{2}$ as $\frac{-1}{2}$.

(*continued on page 52*)

Solution 7.4.1.1

Solution 7.4.1.1

The definition of exp (x) gives

$$\exp(0) = \lim_{k \text{ large}} \left(1 + \frac{0}{k}\right)^k = \lim(1) = 1$$

$$\exp(1) = \lim_{k \text{ large}} \left(1 + \frac{1}{k}\right)^k = e = 2.718$$

$$\exp\left(\frac{1}{10}\right) = \lim_{k \text{ large}} \left(1 + \frac{0.1}{k}\right)^k = 1.105$$

(This last result can be deduced from the table on page 50.)

The first two of these results, exp $(0) = 1$ and exp $(1) = e$, are important. ∎

Solution 7.4.1.2

Solution 7.4.1.2

(i) $u_k = \left(1 + \dfrac{r}{200}\right)^2 u_{k-1}$

(ii) $u_k = \left(1 + \dfrac{r}{400}\right)^4 u_{k-1}$

(iii) $u_k = \left(1 + \dfrac{r}{1200}\right)^{12} u_{k-1}$ ∎

(continued from page 51)

This means, for example, that

$$\exp(-1) = e^{-1} = \frac{1}{e}$$

that

$$\exp(\tfrac{1}{2}) = e^{1/2} = \sqrt{e}$$

and so on.

Exercise 1

Exercise 1
(3 minutes)

Evaluate exp (2), working to two significant figures, using Equation (1) and the information contained in this text only. ∎

The general statement of the exponential theorem is

$$\exp(x) = e^x \quad (x \in R)$$

Main Text
* * *
Equation (2)
* * *

Even assuming that it is not difficult to prove the result expressed by Equation (1), there is an important new point in Equation (2): What do we mean by e^x when x is irrational? Since exp (x) is defined for all real x, we can use Equation (2) to give meaning to e^x. That is, for rational x we prove the result in Equation (2), and for irrational x we *define* e^x by Equation (2).

It is worth noticing that if x and y are rationals it follows from Equation (2) that

$$\exp(x + y) = e^{x+y} = e^x e^y = \exp(x)\exp(y)$$

by the laws of indices. In fact, the equation

$$\exp(x + y) = \exp(x)\exp(y)$$

Equation (3)
* * *

holds for *all* real numbers x and y; we prove this in Appendix II.

Using the language of *Unit 3, Operations and Morphisms*, this result says that exp is a morphism of $(R, +)$ to $(R^+, \times)$, and the graph of the exponential function (on page 51) shows that this morphism is, in fact, an isomorphism.

7.4.3 Natural Logarithms

We have seen how to define e^x for irrational x. How do we define a^x, where a is some real positive number other than e? One way to do it is to find a real number b such that

$$a = e^b = \exp(b)$$

Equation (1)

and then (remembering the laws of indices) to define

$$a^x = (e^b)^x = e^{bx} = \exp(bx)$$

Equation (2)
* * *

To evaluate a^x, therefore, we need the real number b; that is, we must solve Equation (1) by reversing the function exp. Just as the reverse of the function $x \longmapsto 10^x$ is a function called the logarithm to base 10, so the reverse of the function $\exp: x \longmapsto e^x$ is called the logarithm to base e or natural logarithm. The first tables of logarithms, made by John Napier in 1614, were tables of natural logarithms. The symbol for the natural logarithm function is ln (or sometimes $\log_e$ or just log).

The graph of the exponential function, given again below, shows exp to be a one-one function with domain R and codomain R^+. Its reverse, the natural logarithm function, is therefore its inverse and a one-one mapping too, i.e. it is a function. Its graph is shown below. Notice how either graph can be obtained from the other by interchanging the x and y axes. This is a general characteristic of inverse and reverse mappings.

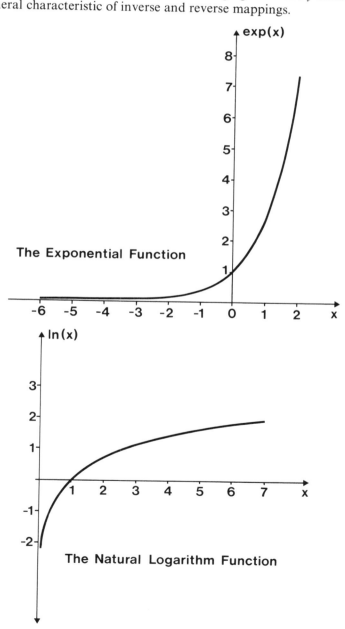

The Exponential Function

The Natural Logarithm Function

(continued on page 54)

Solution 7.4.2.1

Solution 7.4.2.1

$$\exp(2) = e^2$$

$$= (2.72)^2$$

$$= 7.4 \text{ to the required accuracy}$$

(The true value is 7.39 to two decimal places.) ■

(continued from page 53)

Exercise 1

  (i) From the graphs given above, what are the domain and codomain of ln?
 (ii) If $\ln(z) = \ln(x) + \ln(y)$, express z in terms of x and y.
(iii) Evaluate $\ln(e)$. ■

7.4.4 Summary

In this section we introduced the exponential function by discussing population growth; this led us to define

$$\exp : x \longmapsto \lim_{k\,\text{large}} \left(1 + \frac{x}{k}\right)^k \quad (x \in R)$$

which has domain R and codomain R^+. We then stated the exponential theorem:

$$\exp(x) = e^x, \text{ where } e = \exp(1)$$

It follows by the laws of indices that

$$\exp(x + y) = \exp(x)\exp(y)$$

We then defined the reverse of the exponential function, which is a function with domain R^+ and codomain R, called the natural logarithm function. We remarked that this function enables us to define a^x, where $a \in R^+$, for all real values of x.

7.5 APPENDICES (NOT PART OF THE COURSE)

7.5.1 Appendix I

Proof that, if u and v converge, then $u + v$ converges and has the limit $\lim u + \lim v$.

(i) "u is convergent" means that we can find $N \in Z^+$ such that u_k is as close to $\lim u$ as we please for all $k > N$.

(ii) "v is convergent" means that we can find $M \in Z^+$ such that v_k is as close to $\lim v$ as we please for all $k > M$.

We wish to show that we can find $P \in Z^+$ such that $u_k + v_k$ is an approximation to $\lim u + \lim v$ with absolute error bound less than or equal to ε, for any small positive number ε, and for all $k > P$.

We are *adding* the approximation u_k to $\lim u$ to the approximation v_k to $\lim v$ to obtain the approximation $u_k + v_k$ to $\lim u + \lim v$.

In *Unit 2, Errors and Accuracy*, we saw that the absolute error bound for a sum of approximations is equal to the sum of the absolute error bounds of the individual approximations.

We therefore require that the sum of the absolute error bounds of the two approximations be $\leqslant \varepsilon$. There is no reason for one of the absolute error bounds to be less than the other, so we take them to be equal.

By (i), we can find $N \in Z^+$ such that the approximation u_k to $\lim u$ has absolute error bound $\leqslant \dfrac{\varepsilon}{2}$ for all $k > N$: that is

$$u_k \in [\lim u - \tfrac{1}{2}\varepsilon, \lim u + \tfrac{1}{2}\varepsilon] \quad \text{when } k > N$$

By (ii), we can find $M \in Z^+$ such that the approximation v_k to $\lim v$ has absolute error bound $\leqslant \dfrac{\varepsilon}{2}$ for all $k > M$; that is

$$v_k \in [\lim v - \tfrac{1}{2}\varepsilon, \lim v + \tfrac{1}{2}\varepsilon] \quad \text{when } k > M$$

Let P be the larger of M and N. The last two statements together imply that

$$u_k + v_k \in [\lim u + \lim v - \varepsilon, \lim u + \lim v + \varepsilon] \quad \text{for all } k > P$$

which is what we wished to prove, as this statement is true for *any* choice of ε.

Solution 7.4.3.1

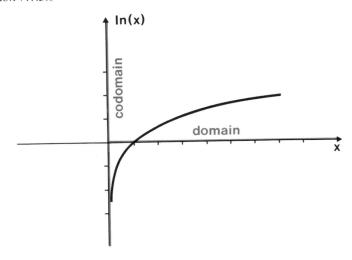

(i) Domain R^+, codomain R.

This can be seen from the graph. Since ln is the inverse of exp, its domain is the image set of exp: $\exp(x)$ gets very small when x is large and negative, but it is never actually zero. The domain of ln is therefore R^+: only positive numbers have logarithms. The codomain of ln is the domain of exp, and is therefore R.

(ii) $$z = xy$$

To find z, given $\ln(z)$, we apply the inverse mapping exp which gives

$$z = \exp(\ln(z)) \qquad \text{by definition of ln}$$
$$= \exp(\ln(x) + \ln(y)) \qquad \text{by given data}$$
$$= \exp(\ln(x)) \times \exp(\ln(y)) \qquad \text{by Equation 7.4.2.3}$$
$$= xy \qquad \text{by definition of ln}$$

This result expresses the fact that ln is a morphism of $(R^+, \times)$ to $(R, +)$: a result we would expect, since we have already noted that exp is an isomorphism, and in *Unit 3, Operations and Morphisms* we noted that the inverse of an isomorphism is an isomorphism.

(iii) $$\ln(e) = \ln(\exp(1)) \qquad \text{by definition of } e$$
$$= 1 \qquad \text{by definition of ln} \qquad \blacksquare$$

7.5.2 Appendix II

Proof that $\lim\limits_{k\,\text{large}} \left(1 + \dfrac{x}{k}\right)^k$ *exists.*

We consider two cases, according to the sign of x.

<u>Case 1 : $x \geqslant 0$</u>

We show that the elements of the sequence $k \longmapsto \left(1 + \dfrac{x}{k}\right)^k$ increase as k increases, and yet never exceed a fixed real number (such a fixed number is called an upper bound), so that the sequence must converge. By the binomial theorem we have

$$\left(1 + \frac{x}{k}\right)^k = 1 + \frac{kx}{k} + \frac{k(k-1)}{k^2}\frac{x^2}{2!} + \frac{k(k-1)(k-2)}{k^3}\frac{x^3}{3!} + \cdots$$
$$+ \frac{k(k-1)\ldots 1}{k^k}\frac{x^k}{k!}$$

$$= 1 + x + \left(1 - \frac{1}{k}\right)\frac{x^2}{2!} + \left(1 - \frac{1}{k}\right)\left(1 - \frac{2}{k}\right)\frac{x^3}{3!} + \cdots$$
$$+ \left(1 - \frac{1}{k}\right)\cdots\left(1 - \frac{k-1}{k}\right)\frac{x^k}{k!}$$

If k is increased then the coefficient of each power of x increases, and in addition some new terms are added to the polynomial which are positive for positive x; so $\left(1 + \dfrac{x}{k}\right)^k$ increases with k. To show that the elements of the sequence are bounded, let N be any integer greater than x; then for $k > N$ the above formula for $\left(1 + \dfrac{x}{k}\right)^k$ gives

$$\left(1 + \frac{x}{k}\right)^k \leqslant 1 + x + \frac{x^2}{2!} + \frac{x^3}{3!} + \cdots + \frac{x^N}{N!} + \frac{x^{N+1}}{(N+1)!}$$
$$+ \frac{x^{N+2}}{(N+2)!} + \cdots + \frac{x^k}{k!}$$

$$= \left(1 + x + \frac{x^2}{2!} + \frac{x^3}{3!} + \cdots + \frac{x^N}{N!}\right)$$
$$\times \left(1 + \frac{x}{N+1} + \frac{x^2}{(N+1)(N+2)} + \cdots + \frac{x^{k-N}}{(N+1)\ldots k}\right)$$

$$\leqslant \left(1 + x + \frac{x^2}{2!} + \frac{x^3}{3!} + \cdots + \frac{x^N}{N!}\right)$$
$$\times \left(1 + \frac{x}{N} + \frac{x^2}{N^2} + \cdots + \frac{x^{k-N}}{N^{k-N}}\right)$$

$$= 1 + x + \frac{x^2}{2!} + \frac{x^3}{3!} + \cdots + \frac{x^N}{N!}\left(\frac{1 - \left(\dfrac{x}{N}\right)^{k-N+1}}{1 - \left(\dfrac{x}{N}\right)}\right)$$

(after summing the geometric progression)

$$\leqslant 1 + x + \frac{x^2}{2!} + \frac{x^2}{3!} + \cdots + \frac{x^N}{N!}\left(\frac{1}{1 - \left(\dfrac{x}{N}\right)}\right)$$

(since $N > x$ and $x \geqslant 0$)

which is independent of k, and is therefore an upper bound on every element of the sequence. There is a theorem, which we shall not prove here, that any sequence whose elements increase with k but have an upper bound must converge. By this theorem, therefore, the sequence $\left(1 + \dfrac{x}{k}\right)^k$ converges for $x \geq 0$.

Case II: $x < 0$

We can prove the convergence of the sequence defining $\exp(x)$ as a by-product of the following result, which also serves to prove the multiplication theorem for the exponential function:

$$\exp(y - z) = \frac{\exp(y)}{\exp(z)} \qquad \text{Equation (1)}$$

i.e. the sequence $k \longmapsto \left(1 + \dfrac{(y - z)}{k}\right)^k$ converges and its limit is $\dfrac{\exp(y)}{\exp(z)}$.

To show this we consider the expression

$$\frac{\left(1 + \dfrac{y - z}{k}\right)^k \left(1 + \dfrac{z}{k}\right)^k}{\left(1 + \dfrac{y}{k}\right)^k} = \left(\frac{1 + \dfrac{y}{k} + \dfrac{(y - z)z}{k^2}}{1 + \dfrac{y}{k}}\right)^k = \left(1 + \frac{\theta_k}{k}\right)^k \qquad \text{Equation (2)}$$

where y and z are positive or zero, and

$$\theta_k = \frac{(y - z)z}{k\left(1 + \dfrac{y}{k}\right)} \quad (k = 1, 2, \ldots)$$

The binomial expansion gives

$$\left(1 + \frac{\theta_k}{k}\right)^k - 1 = k\left(\frac{\theta_k}{k}\right) + \frac{k(k - 1)}{2}\left(\frac{\theta_k}{k}\right)^2 + \cdots + \left(\frac{\theta_k}{k}\right)^k,$$

and so

$$\left|\left(1 + \frac{\theta_k}{k}\right)^k - 1\right| \leq |\theta_k| + |\theta_k|^2 + \cdots + |\theta_k|^k$$

$$= |\theta_k|\left(\frac{1 - |\theta_k|^k}{1 - |\theta_k|}\right) \leq \frac{|\theta_k|}{1 - |\theta_k|}$$

provided that $|\theta_k| < 1$.

The definition of θ_k implies that $\lim\limits_{k \text{ large}}(\theta_k) = 0$ and hence that $\dfrac{|\theta_k|}{1 - |\theta_k|}$ can be made as small as we please by making k large enough. Consequently, $\left|\left(1 + \dfrac{\theta_k}{k}\right)^k - 1\right|$ can also be made as small as we please; and so the limit of the sequence $\left(1 + \dfrac{\theta_k}{k}\right)^k$ is 1. It follows, by the multiplication rule for limits and by Equation (2), that

$$\lim_{k \text{ large}}\left(1 + \frac{y - z}{k}\right)^k = \frac{\lim\limits_{k \text{ large}}\left(1 + \dfrac{y}{k}\right)^k \lim\limits_{k \text{ large}}\left(1 + \dfrac{\theta_k}{k}\right)^k}{\lim\limits_{k \text{ large}}\left(1 + \dfrac{z}{k}\right)^k}$$

(Note that the denominator is non-zero.)

so

$$\exp(y - z) = \frac{\exp(y)}{\exp(z)}$$

We can use this result in two ways. First, taking $y = 0$ and z positive, we have a proof that the sequence defining $\exp(z)$ for negative values of z converges, and that its limit is the reciprocal of $\exp(-z)$. That is,

$$\exp(-z) = \frac{1}{\exp(z)}$$

Equation (3)

Secondly, we can use it to prove the result:

$$\exp(x_1)\exp(x_2) = \exp(x_1 + x_2)$$

Equation (4)

by substituting, e.g., $y = x_1 + x_2$, $z = x_1$ in Equation (1), where $x_1 \geqslant 0$ and $x_2 \geqslant 0$.

7.5.3 Appendix III

Proof of The Exponential Theorem

The proof of Equation 7.4.2.1 depends on a preliminary result, or *lemma*, a demonstration of which we set as an exercise. You can use it to test your understanding of sequences.

Exercise 1

Given that x is a real number and k is a positive integer, demonstrate, by writing out the sequence defining $\exp(x)$ and the sequence consisting of the kth powers of the elements in the sequence defining $\exp\left(\dfrac{x}{k}\right)$, the lemma

$$\exp(x) = \left(\exp\left(\frac{x}{k}\right)\right)^k$$

Try $k = 2$ first (since there is nothing to demonstrate when $k = 1$). ■

The lemma you have just demonstrated,

$$\exp x = \left(\exp\left(\frac{x}{k}\right)\right)^k \quad (x \in R \text{ and } k \in Z^+)$$

can be used in two ways. First we set $x = k = p$ and obtain

$$\exp(p) = (\exp(1))^p = e^p \quad (p \in Z^+)$$

Secondly, we set $x = p$ and $k = q$ in the same result, with p and q both positive integers, obtaining

$$\exp(p) = \left(\exp\left(\frac{p}{q}\right)\right)^q \quad (p, q \in Z^+)$$

Substituting for $\exp(p)$ and then interchanging the two sides of the equation:

$$\left(\exp\left(\frac{p}{q}\right)\right)^q = e^p \quad (p, q \in Z^+)$$

Finally, taking the qth root of both sides, we obtain

$$\exp\left(\frac{p}{q}\right) = \sqrt[q]{e^p}$$

$$= e^{p/q} \text{ by the laws of indices.}$$

This is equivalent to the statement that

$$\exp(x) = e^x$$

Equation (1)

when x is positive and rational. This result cries out to be generalized to

(*continued on page 60*)

Solution 1   **Solution 1**

The sequence defining exp (x) is

$$1 + x, \quad (1 + \tfrac{1}{2}x)^2, \quad (1 + \tfrac{1}{3}x)^3, \quad (1 + \tfrac{1}{4}x)^4, \dots$$

For $k = 2$, the sequence defining $\exp\left(\dfrac{x}{k}\right)$ is

$$1 + \tfrac{1}{2}x, \quad (1 + \tfrac{1}{4}x)^2, \quad (1 + \tfrac{1}{6}x)^3, \dots$$

and so, since $(\lim u)^2 = \lim (u^2)$ by the multiplication rule for limits, $\left(\exp\left(\dfrac{x}{2}\right)\right)^2$ is the limit of the sequence

$$(1 + \tfrac{1}{2}x)^2, \quad (1 + \tfrac{1}{4}x)^4, \dots$$

This sequence consists of alternate elements from the first sequence above; and since the terms $\left(1 + \dfrac{x}{n}\right)^n$ for n large in the first sequence are all close to its limit, the ones which appear in the last sequence are close to this limit, and so the last sequence has the same limit as the first. This demonstrates that

$$\left(\exp\left(\dfrac{x}{2}\right)\right)^2 = \exp(x)$$

For a general positive integer k, the demonstration is analogous; in place of the last sequence we get

$$\left(1 + \dfrac{1}{k}x\right)^k, \quad \left(1 + \dfrac{1}{2k}x\right)^{2k}, \dots$$

which consists of every kth term from the first sequence and therefore has the same limit. ∎

(*continued from page 59*)

negative values and irrational values of x. The generalization to negative values depends on a theorem

$$\exp(x) \times \exp(y) = \exp(x + y) \quad (x \in R \text{ and } y \in R)$$ Equation (2)

whose proof is given in Appendix II. If x is negative and rational, we put $y = -x$ and so Equations (1) and (2) give

$$\exp(x) = \frac{\exp(0)}{\exp(y)}$$

$$= \frac{1}{e^y} \text{ by Equation (1)} \quad (\text{since } y > 0)$$

$$= e^{-y} = e^x$$

This proves the exponential theorem for negative rational x.

The generalization of the exponential theorem to irrational values of x depends on how we define e^x. If x is rational, it can be put in the form $\dfrac{p}{q}$ with p and q integers, and then e^x means $e^{p/q}$, that is the qth root of e^p; but we have no corresponding definition for irrational values of x. The problem for irrational x, therefore, is not how to prove Equation (2) but how to define e^x; the natural answer is to adopt Equation (2) as our definition of e^x for irrational x. Combining our previous results with this definition for irrational x, we end up with the important result

$$\exp(x) = e^x \quad (x \in R)$$ Equation (3)

which is the *exponential theorem*.

Unit No.		Title of Text
1		Functions
2		Errors and Accuracy
3		Operations and Morphisms
4		Finite Differences
5	NO TEXT	
6		Inequalities
7		Sequences and Limits I
8		Computing I
9		Integration I
10	NO TEXT	
11		Logic I — Boolean Algebra
12		Differentiation I
13		Integration II
14		Sequences and Limits II
15		Differentiation II
16		Probability and Statistics I
17		Logic II — Proof
18		Probability and Statistics II
19		Relations
20		Computing II
21		Probability and Statistics III
22		Linear Algebra I
23		Linear Algebra II
24		Differential Equations I
25	NO TEXT	
26		Linear Algebra III
27		Complex Numbers I
28		Linear Algebra IV
29		Complex Numbers II
30		Groups I
31		Differential Equations II
32	NO TEXT	
33		Groups II
34		Number Systems
35		Topology
36		Mathematical Structures